PRAISE FOR

A Garden of Friends

A Garden of Friends not only teaches us how to cultivate new
and beautiful relationships, but it also encourages us to enjoy the unique
fragrance of the friendships already growing in our lives.

LENYA HEITZIG
Pastor's wife
Award-winning Author and Speaker

Thank you, Penny, for all that you do to inspire and
encourage women in their walk with Christ.

JONI EARECKSON TADA

A Garden of Friends

Penny Pierce Rose

Regal

From Gospel Light
Ventura, California, U.S.A.

PUBLISHED BY REGAL BOOKS
FROM GOSPEL LIGHT
VENTURA, CALIFORNIA, U.S.A.
PRINTED IN THE U.S.A.

Regal Books is a ministry of Gospel Light, a Christian publisher dedicated to serving the local church. We believe God's vision for Gospel Light is to provide church leaders with biblical, user-friendly materials that will help them evangelize, disciple and minister to children, youth and families.

It is our prayer that this Regal book will help you discover biblical truth for your own life and help you meet the needs of others. May God richly bless you.

For a free catalog of resources from Regal Books/Gospel Light, please call your Christian supplier or contact us at 1-800-4-GOSPEL or www.regalbooks.com.

Published in association with the literary agency of fm Management, 24981 Dana Point Harbor Dr., Suite 110, Dana Point, CA 92629.

Library of Congress Cataloging-in-Publication Data
Rose, Penny Pierce.
  A garden of friends / Penny Pierce Rose.
    p. cm.
  ISBN 0-8307-3706-5 (hardcover)
  1. Female friendship—Religious aspects—Christianity. 2. Christian women—Religious life. 3. Flowers—Religious aspects—Christianity. 4. Flowers—Miscellanea. I. Title.
  BV4527.R66 2005
  241'.6762'082—dc22   2005018086

1   2   3   4   5   6   7   8   9   10   /   10   09   08   07   06   05

Rights for publishing this book in other languages are contracted by Gospel Light Worldwide, the international nonprofit ministry of Gospel Light. Gospel Light Worldwide also provides publishing and technical assistance to international publishers dedicated to producing Sunday School and Vacation Bible School curricula and books in the languages of the world. For additional information, visit www.gospellightworld-wide.org; write to Gospel Light Worldwide, P.O. Box 3875, Ventura, CA 93006; or send an e-mail to info@gospellightworldwide.org.

Contents

Acknowledgments

This book was written in honor of my garden of friends past, present and future. Without you my life would, indeed, be a desert. Thanks to so many of you for praying me through this project.

I also owe a debt of gratitude (and many home-cooked meals) to my family—Kerry, Erin, Kristina and Ryan—who willingly and lovingly allowed me to spend time in the writing cave. You're the best! Also, thanks to my parents who supported me throughout this project and picked up the slack for me. I'm so grateful God planted me in your garden.

Most important, I dedicate this book to the Friend who has loved me through every season of my life: Jesus Christ.

The Garden in My Heart

Knowing that five-year-old Lizzie was terrified of lightning and thunder, Lizzie's mom went into her daughter's room during a thunderstorm, sat on the bed beside the sniffling girl and said, "Don't be afraid, Lizzie, God is right here in the room with you."

Trying to be brave, the little girl replied, "Okay, Mommy, I won't be afraid."

Her mom kissed her goodnight and left to get ready for bed. Suddenly, lightning clapped, thunder rolled and Lizzie screamed bloody murder. Her mom ran to comfort her daughter and said, "Honey, I thought you weren't going to be afraid. Remember? God is here in the room with you."

"I know God is here, Mommy, but right now I need someone with skin on!"

At one time or another, every one of us has felt like little Lizzie—we just need someone with skin on! For girls, their friends can be their best "skin on" companions. An article in *Ladies' Home Journal* explains a key truth concerning girls: For us, friends are everything.

It would be hard to exaggerate, especially for girls, just how critical their girlfriends are in their lives. As a parent, you'll sometimes feel—if you haven't already—that you're less important to your daughter than her 12 best friends. In a certain way—take a deep breath—this is true.[1]

Do you remember when you had the luxury of thinking that your girlfriends were everything? Now that I am an adult, God, my husband and my children have taken their rightful priority, and my friends have sometimes taken a backseat. But when I reflect on my entire life, I realize that I haven't marked the passage of time in terms of what year it was or who was president, or any of the other milestones people use to keep track of history. I mark time according to who was my "best friend."

Count your age with friends but not with years.

ANONYMOUS

My childhood best friend was Susan.[2] She was a girl's girl. She had a thick blonde braid trailing down her back and owned a closet full of frilly clothes. She had her very own piano and a pink-and-white playhouse in her front yard stocked with dishes, furniture and every doll and accessory imaginable. Susan was a breath of fresh air. I could escape the maleness of a house dominated by brothers and take refuge in a totally female-friendly environment, where tea parties weren't interrupted by war cries and playing dress-up wasn't grounds for merciless teasing.

When we were in third grade, Susan's mother died of cancer. I remember walking by the coffin at the funeral, warily peeking over as I grasped my mother's hand for support. I remember helping my grandmother lay out food in the Fellowship Hall after the service, thinking, *Why are we making a party out of this?* That day, Susan came home with me. I don't know how we did

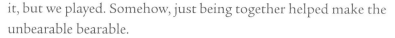

it, but we played. Somehow, just being together helped make the unbearable bearable.

My middle school best friend was the "dangerous" Toni. She snuck cigarettes out to the garage and urged me to take a puff; she'd leave home without telling her parents and show up at my house without warning; she'd wear acceptable clothes out of the house and change into outrageous attire when she got to my house. From Toni I learned that actions have consequences. When my parents smelled smoke on my breath, I was grounded for a month.

A chain of friends links me to my past like a wreath of flowers: Kathy, the clownish girl who hid painful family secrets behind a smiling mask; Janine, the beautiful bombshell who never wanted for a date but never felt worthy of love; and Catrina, the tough but tender girl who looked for love in all the wrong places. Each of these friends has informed who I am as an adult and, thankfully, our paths still cross during the holidays, at class reunions or when something reminds us to reach across the distance. When we see one another, our love and affection is still palpable. We easily remember why we were best friends.

As an adult, my friends are just as intricately linked in my heart and mind. We share the struggles, triumphs, tears and laughter of adulthood. Often our children or husbands bring us to friendship. We'll sit at baseball games and solve the world's problems as we cheer on our kid's teams. At stuffy dinner parties we'll giggle at private jokes no one else would understand. At church, we look across the aisle and feel safe knowing that we have a friend who knows all about us and loves us anyway. I look at these special women—these "skin on" companions—as my garden of friends. The years have taught me that friends are a God-given treasure. I believe that He purposely plants people as a garden in our hearts to teach us how to care for and cultivate loving relationships.

The Garden in My Heart

In my mind's eye, when I wander through my garden of friends, I notice several prevalent features that characterize them. I'm sure your friends share some or all of these same characteristics:

- Loveliness
- Uniqueness
- Selflessness
- Neediness

Loveliness

Each of my friends is beautiful. Some have short hair, some have long hair; some let their hair go gray, and others . . . well, let's just say, only their hairdresser knows for sure. I have friends of all shapes, sizes, colors and ages. But there are times when I'm with my friends that their loveliness takes my breath away. It could be a mischievous glint in the eye, a slightly crooked smile or a flair for fashion that only hints at the inner beauty of the women I call my friends. Who they are on the inside blossoms on the outside. I admit that not many of my friends look like movie stars or fashion models; but like multicolored flowers in a garden, my friends are beautiful inside and out.

Uniqueness

Just as there are many types of plants and flowers in a garden, there are also different kinds of people whom I feel privileged to call friends. No two of my friends look alike, think alike or have the same personality. Some work outside the home; several are stay-at-home wives and mothers; others are involved in philanthropic enterprises. Some of my friends love politics, while others don't even watch the news. Some are exercise freaks who don't mind hanging out with couch potatoes like me. Each of my friends is unlike any other; each adds color, fragrance and joy to my life through her individual perspective and personality.

Selflessness

My friends have busy, consuming lives, yet they take time to show their care for me. I think of the phone calls that have come at just the right moment with a steady voice saying, "I just thought you needed to know I'm praying for you." Every so often a friend will e-mail a joke or an encouraging quote to say, in effect, "You are loved." When I've been lambasted by a migraine, I've had friends drop everything to take me to the emergency room. Following surgery, 12 of my friends got together and fed my family for a month. Amazingly, one of the most elaborate dinners was offered by the lady who could least afford it. You see, true friends find joy in giving 'til it hurts.

A friend is one who knows you as you are, understands where you've been, accepts who you've become and still gently invites you to grow.

ANONYMOUS

Neediness

Not to say that my friends are perfect—I will admit that my friends have a bit of neediness. However, as different flowers require specific methods of care, no two of my friends expect the same attention from me. One may need a phone call every day while another only needs sparse contact to remain intertwined. While they may not be perfect, they are *my* friends. They're the women God has planted in my garden; and it is my joy to cultivate their friendships, whether they are independent or needy, depressed or delighted, somber or smiling.

In God's Garden

My idea of a friend is a person whom I love and trust; a close companion; someone who walks beside me through good times and bad. The Bible recounts the stories of some of God's friends but, more importantly, reveals that God Himself wants to become friends with mere mortals. And He exhibits the characteristics of a good friend. In fact, He is the perfect embodiment of a best friend.

God's Loveliness

Scripture tells us that, like our human friends, He is lovely. The Song of Solomon describes Him this way: "He is altogether lovely. This is my beloved, and this is my friend" (Song of Sol. 5:16). When I think of God's loveliness, I'm reminded of these lines from a song: "You are beautiful beyond description, too marvelous for words."[3] There are times spent in His presence in worship or prayer when I can sense His beauty surrounding me, taking my breath away.

> *Let us be grateful to people who make us happy; they are the charming gardeners who make our souls blossom.*
>
> MARCEL PROUST

God's Uniqueness

Not only is God lovely, He is also unique. King David, another human who was loved by God, reveled in God's matchlessness: "You are great, O Lord GOD. For *there is none like You*, nor is there any God besides You, according to all that we have heard with our ears" (2 Sam. 7:22, emphasis added). Can anyone or anything compare to God? He created all things, He has power over all things, and He knows all things. How astounding that this unique God knows everything about us and loves us anyway.

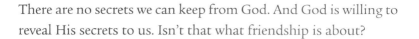

There are no secrets we can keep from God. And God is willing to reveal His secrets to us. Isn't that what friendship is about?

God's Selflessness

God, the lovely and unique One, has proven to be completely selfless. He even went so far as to give His only Son over to death to pay the price for the sins of His friends: "For God so loved the world that He gave His only begotten Son, that whoever believes in Him should not perish but have everlasting life" (John 3:16). Jesus said, "Greater love has no one than this, than to lay down one's life for his friends" (John 15:13). God Himself gave His life for the friends He so dearly loves.

God's Self-Sufficiency

Unlike our human friends, God is completely self-sufficient. He doesn't need anything or anyone. But He does greatly long for His creatures to know Him and to develop a personal relationship with Him, now and in eternity. In His prayer for believers, Jesus expressed this longing: "Father, I desire that they also whom You gave Me may be with Me where I am, that they may behold My glory which You have given Me; for You loved Me before the foundation of the world" (John 17:24). How amazing that we have been given to Christ to become His friends and to behold His glory! As Jesus said to His disciples, "No longer do I call you servants, for a servant does not know what his master is doing; but I have called you friends" (John 15:15).

How Does Your Garden Grow?

I imagine that reading about my "skin on" friends has brought some of your friends to mind. Why don't you take a mental stroll through your girlhood garden of friends? Think about the girl who was your childhood friend and how she helped you to grow into the person you are today. Perhaps you were a serious child and she taught you to laugh. Perhaps she didn't have as many material possessions as you, so she taught you to be grateful for what you had been given. Maybe she was academically gifted and encouraged you to study harder than you would have otherwise. Doubtless, you can still catch a wisp of her fragrance in your life.

Now think about your adolescent "best friends." Were they daredevils or darlings? Did they teach you how to wear makeup or help you get in touch with your inner athlete? Put yourself back in your teenaged shoes and remember the devotion and emotion you poured into your girlfriends.

Throughout this book, you'll want to reflect on the women who surround you and discover which flower each one is in your garden of friends. We'll learn together the characteristics, care and cultivation of the fabulous women God has planted in your life.

Most importantly, spend some time thinking about how God became your friend. Did you embrace His friendship early or later in life? Did He come into your heart during a time of upheaval, or did you slowly become aware of His desire to know you intimately? Do you consider Him your best friend?

Perhaps you haven't accepted God's offer of friendship. Know that He longs to include you in *His* garden of friends, to transplant you into His kingdom. To become God's friend, you don't have to join a special group or live in a certain neighborhood. Scripture tells us, "Draw near to God and He will draw near to you" (Jas. 4:8). Allow me to walk you through some simple steps to friendship with God.

Follow His Call

When Jesus first met His disciples, He didn't ask for personal references or credentials. He simply said, "Follow Me" (Matt. 4:19).

The word "follow" conveys the meaning of walking beside another, going in the same direction, or accompanying a person to their destination. But to follow also carries the idea of pursuing another with determination and persistence, like children intent on following the leader.[4] When God calls us to follow Him, He's asking us to walk beside Him in loving companionship; but He *is* willing to take the lead and show us the way to go. I don't know about you, but if I'm lost, I'd much rather have someone guide me than give me directions and send me out on my own. That's what God does—not only does He come alongside us, but He also goes before us.

Believe God's Promise

"To believe" means "to be persuaded or to place one's confidence in something or someone."[5] In Scripture, to believe means to trust in Christ for salvation. Paul promised, "If you confess with your mouth the Lord Jesus and believe in your heart that God has raised Him from the dead, you will be saved" (Rom. 10:9). You see, God put on skin and came to the world as the man Jesus Christ so that you could be spared judgment. Jesus died on the cross to pay the price for your sins so that you can live with Him in eternity. That's a promise worth clinging to!

> *Every experience God gives us, every person he puts in our lives, is the perfect preparation for the future that only he can see.*
>
> CORRIE TEN BOOM

Trust God's Plan

"'I know the plans I have for you,' declares the LORD, 'plans to prosper you and not to harm you, plans to give you hope and a future'" (Jer. 29:11, *NIV*). Sometimes the future can seem murky or frightening. But God—your friend—has your best interests at heart, and He really does have a wonderful plan for your life. Even in the tough times, you can count on God to be the "friend who sticks closer than a brother" (Prov. 18:24).

As you contemplate your garden of friends and learn to better cultivate your relationships with them, remember that the best friend you'll ever have is God. Purpose in your heart to be a friend of God. When you become His friend, He'll help make your earthly friendships blossom.

For his doctoral thesis, a college student spent a year with a group of Navajo Indians on a reservation in the Southwest. As part of his research, he lived with a family: sleeping in their home, eating their food, working as they worked and living the life of a Native American. The old grandmother spoke no English, and the college student no Navajo, yet a close friendship formed between the two. In spite of the language difference, they shared a bond of love and understanding. As the months passed, the student learned a few phrases of Navajo and the grandmother picked up some English. When it came time for the student to return home to write his thesis, the tribe held a going-away celebration. As the young man prepared to climb into his pickup truck and drive away, the old grandmother came to bid him a private good-bye. With tears streaming from her eyes, she placed her hands on either side of his face, looked into his eyes and said, "I like me best when I'm with you."[6]

The grandmother's words carry great insight—we tend to *like* ourselves best when we're with our friends. What she may not have understood is that we *become* our best when we spend time with the "friend who sticks closer than a brother" (Prov. 18:24).

Digging Deeper

1. Think of the friends God has planted in your heart's garden. Journal about how they have helped make you into the person you are today.

2. In which of the following ways have you made sacrifices for your friends?

   ❏ Sacrifice of time
   ❏ Sacrifice of emotion
   ❏ Sacrifice of physical energy
   ❏ Sacrifice of prayer
   ❏ Other _____

3. Read John 15:13-14. Then answer the following questions.

What sacrifice did Jesus make to show Himself a faithful friend?

What does He expect in return?

4. Describe how your relationship with God has developed. Use the verbs "follow," "believe" and "trust" to explain the growth of your friendship with God.

5. If you have not asked God to be your friend and if you earnestly desire His friendship, say the following prayer with all your heart:

God, thank You for loving me enough to send
Your Son to die for me. I ask You to come into my heart
to be my friend and Savior. I know that I'm a sinner,
and I ask You to wash me clean and give me a new life in You.
I trust You to be the closest friend I'll ever have. Help me
to be a good friend to You. Amen.

The Master Gardener

Not many things delight the senses like a flower garden: It titillates our sense of smell with the earth's musky aroma and the petals' sweet perfume; it hums with trickling water and buzzing bees. A garden can tickle the fingertips with delicate blossoms or prickly vines; tantalize our eyesight with an abundance of colors, shapes and sizes; and even feed our sweet tooth if we tease the honey from a delicate white bloom.

I have to admit, however, that gardening is not my thing. I don't like to get dirt under my fingernails or endure the glaring sun as I bend over to till soil or deadhead fading flowers. I'd rather sit comfortably on a lawn chair on my porch with a cold iced tea, rising only to meander around the yard and enjoy the beautiful garden in bloom.

I'm fortunate because, while I wouldn't call myself a gardener, my husband, Kerry, loves playing in the dirt. He enjoys planting flowers and pruning bushes—he even gets a kick out of pulling weeds! As far as Kerry is concerned, the ground surrounding our home is always a work in progress; he's constantly getting out the shovel to turn over the soil, to plant and transplant, to shape and reshape the landscape. In his mind's eye, there is always the potential for new growth; he's a gardener in every sense of the word and has made the environment surrounding our house quite enticing.

The Garden in My Heart

This may seem obvious, but to cultivate a garden of friends, we should exhibit the characteristics of a master gardener. Let's face it, friendships, like a garden, are a work in progress; and it takes effort to keep them growing and blooming.

When I searched the Web for information about master gardeners, I learned that they display three characteristics. They are

- Hands on
- Hands off
- Willing to lend a hand

Let's apply these insights to learn the keys to help us cultivate a flourishing garden of friends.

Hands On

No gardener can hope to harvest a crop without getting his or her hands dirty. Gardeners love to dig in the soil, dig out weeds and dig up excess foliage that might hinder their plants from growing. Good friends, godly friends, are like that—they're willing to be hands on and get personally involved.

For example, when I began writing Bible studies for our women's ministry at church, some ladies would say to me, "It's too simple." Others would say, "It's too hard." I knew it could be better, but my critics would only tell me that it wasn't right, not *how* to make it right. Many days I'd go home and weep out of frustration.

Then I met a scholarly English professor named Elizabeth. She said, "Why don't you let me edit your work?" I was thrilled that someone was willing to come along-side me, so I eagerly placed the homework in her capable hands. She graciously didn't write her comments in red ink because she didn't want to hurt my feelings. Instead, she wrote her suggestions in pencil so I wouldn't feel threatened. Even as she dug out passive language, run-on sentences and gaps in logic, Elizabeth planted the gift of encouragement in a very practical way. A hands-on friend should be like that: willing to point out some things we could edit in our lives, while encouraging us in the areas that are pleasing to God.

> *Love is the fairest bloom in God's garden.*
>
> ANONYMOUS

Hands Off

It's important to remember that there are times when a garden-er can be *too* hands on. A good gardener develops the patience to be hands off and let things grow. Not long ago, I walked by a lit-tle sprout in our yard and plucked it out. Kerry came outside and said, "Did you pull up that shoot growing in the corner? I've been watching it for three years to see what it would turn into." Oops! It took him a while to forgive my overeager hands-on approach to his garden.

We can be that way with our friends, too, can't we? So eager to pluck out what we see as weeds growing in their lives that we don't give them a chance to bloom. Let me give you an example. After writing for our women's ministry for several years, it was time for me to mentor another person in writing. Under Elizabeth's tutelage, I felt ready to transplant my knowledge into someone else. My friend Teresa dug in and submitted her first lesson. I marked up the lesson in pencil, so the red wouldn't look like her page was bleeding. Teresa made the changes I asked for, but after a few weeks, quit the writing team saying she felt too confined by the requirements.

Soon after that, she had an article published in a well-known Christian magazine. I realized I had been trying to mold her writing to fit mine and had failed to see the individual style she was developing. I rejoiced at her success, realizing she didn't really need my hands-on editing.

I've discovered that it's good to be willing to dig in the dirt, but we must also be sensitive enough to take a hands-off approach, leaving some things alone and patiently waiting to see what develops.

Willing to Lend a Hand

All of the master gardeners I've encountered are willing to lend a hand. They love to give advice and are often eager to put their knowledge into action. When Kerry praised my Uncle Kenneth's irises, Uncle Kenneth immediately went out into the yard (in his "Sunday best" clothes) to dig up some bulbs for our garden. We now have scads of irises, and if anyone compliments them, you guessed it—Kerry digs up bulbs for them to transplant.

I'm thankful I have good friends who will lend a hand. A few years ago, I attended a writer's conference and became aware that I didn't have some of the Bible study skills necessary to add scriptural depth to the lessons. I told my friend and spiritual mentor, Lenya, "I just don't know how to do it." She replied, "I'll show you." A few days later, I was at her house, sitting beside her at the computer, learning to outline Bible passages and practicing how to research the meanings of words. She poured herself into my spiritual growth, helping me hone my study skills.

Can you imagine what would happen if gardeners weren't willing to lend a hand and share their expertise (as well as their seeds and bulbs)? The world would be a desert. Likewise, if friends were not willing to pour themselves into one another's lives, helping each other to grow and flourish, life would be pretty bleak.

In God's Garden

God On Hand

God initiated relationships in a garden. Everything God created in the Garden of Eden. He considered good. But after creating Adam, He clearly said, "It is *not good* that man should be alone" (Gen. 2:18, emphasis added). Rather than leaving Adam alone to talk to the animals like Dr. Doolittle, God created a companion for this single man. Out of Adam's own flesh, God fashioned the woman Eve for Adam to talk to, laugh with and love (see Gen. 2:22-25).

Not only did God provide companionship for Adam, He Himself also was a friend and companion. God came to meet with Adam and Eve "in the garden in the cool of the day" (Gen. 3:8). It was in this paradise that God established an intimate relationship with His human friends. He spent time with them so that they could know and understand Him. There is every indication that He was a very hands-on friend to them.

God Lending a Hand

Sadly, sin entered the world in the Garden. Scripture tells how Satan, the cunning serpent, came into the Garden to tempt Eve to take a bite of the forbidden fruit, promising that "in the day you eat of it your eyes will be opened, and you will be like God, knowing good and evil" (Gen. 3:5). Disregarding God's direction,

Eve "took of its fruit and ate. She also gave to her husband with her, and he ate" (v. 6). At that point, fellowship with God was broken—Eve and Adam then hid their nakedness from God because they were afraid (see. v. 8). You know the rest of the story: God cursed the disobedient couple and banned them from the Garden, sending them into an inhospitable world (see vv. 14-23). At this point, God became hands off and allowed the couple to suffer the consequences of their disobedience.

Thankfully, God didn't abandon them; He came alongside to lend a hand. In order to resume a relationship with the wayward couple, God conducted the first animal sacrifice to cover their sin: "For Adam and his wife the LORD God made tunics of skin, and clothed them" (Gen. 3:21). Graciously, God willingly lent a hand so that the couple could once again connect with Him.

> *Before God can make the heart into a garden of the Lord, he has to plough it, and that will take away a great deal of natural beauty.*
>
> OSWALD CHAMBERS

God Laying Down His Life

Just like His Father, Jesus cultivated relationships in a garden. It was in the Garden of Gethsemane that "Jesus often met . . . with His disciples" (John 18:2). This garden was a place of friendship and fellowship. Imagine the disciples getting to know Jesus intimately, far away from the crowds. Maybe they had picnics or deep theological discussions. Or maybe they simply sat and enjoyed the serenity of the olive press. Sadly, in this garden Jesus was betrayed to His trial and death by one whom He had called friend. From a garden, Jesus departed to make the ultimate sacrifice so that all who believed could experience intimacy with God.

Victoriously, it was in a garden that God displayed His power over death. Jesus was buried in the garden tomb and laid there for three days (see John 19:41). But on the third day, He arose, ultimately to ascend to the Father's right hand.

And one day, Jesus will come back to Earth and take us to live with Him in paradise. The Greek word for paradise literally means "an Eden."[1] We will live with God in a perfect place where we can "eat from the tree of life, which is in the midst of the Paradise of God" (Rev. 2:7). How beautiful that much of salvation's story finds its setting in gardens.

God does indeed love gardens; but more than gardens, God loves godly relationships—He is a gardener of people. Isaiah 5:1 reveals that God delights in tending His people, "Now let me sing to my Well-beloved a song of my Beloved regarding His vineyard: My Well-beloved has a vineyard on a very fruitful hill. He dug it up and cleared out its stones, and planted it with the choicest vine." God, our Beloved Well-Beloved, is a fruitful gardener of people, even if it means digging up, clearing out and planting new life in His people's hearts. As the Master Gardener worked in Eve and Adam's life, He works in ours: digging up sin, clearing the way to intimacy by covering our sins and planting new life in our hearts.

How Does Your Garden Grow?

Growing up I was told, "Your grandmother was born with a green thumb." While I didn't inherit the gardening DNA from Mima, I love to grow personal relationships and pray to have a friendship "green thumb."

As children of God, we can inherit the qualities of God, the Master Gardener, when we allow His Holy Spirit to work in our lives. I believe that only through the power of the Holy Spirit can our garden of friends grow and flourish.

In the same way that friends pour themselves into one another's lives, helping each other to grow and change, once you accept Jesus Christ as your Savior, God pours the Holy Spirit into your heart, creating a whole new you. Scripture tells us that "if anyone is in Christ, he is a new creation; old things have passed away; behold, all things have become new" (2 Cor. 5:17). Your old way of building relationships can become a thing of the past. Once God's Spirit has been implanted into your soul, you can become like the Master Gardener and cultivate friendships His way. Paul told the Corinthians, "As the Spirit of the Lord works within us, we become more and more like him and reflect his glory even more" (2 Cor. 3:18, *NLT*). God sends the Holy Spirit to till the soil in our hearts so that we can become like Him. Simply put, what He is to us, we can be to others.

Helping Others

One way the Spirit reveals Himself is as "the Helper" (John 14:26). Jesus explained the Helper's role to the disciples: "He will teach you all things, and bring to your remembrance all things that I said to you" (John 14:26-27). The Holy Spirit is on hand, reminding us to pass on Christ's words of hope and healing to others.

Is there someone in your life who needs help? The greatest help you can give her is more than physical—it's spiritual. By pointing your friend to the Helper, you're giving her the greatest resource of all. Try taking a hands-on approach with a friend in need by studying the Bible and praying with her; you'll draw closer to one another and to God.

Giving God Room to Move

Scripture teaches that the Holy Spirit is also the One to "convict the world of sin, and of righteousness, and of judgment" (John

16:8). It could be that you have a friend you need to turn over to God. Perhaps you've been so hands on that you've failed to give God room to move. It's good to remember that God is God and we're not! It's simply not our responsibility to be the Holy Spirit in our friend's lives. Sometimes the best way to help a friend is to take a hands-off approach and turn her over in prayer to God.

You'll be amazed at the perfect way God moves when you patiently pray and wait upon His Spirit to work in her life—and you can be sure He'll be working in yours, too.

Plant a seed of friendship; reap a bouquet of happiness.

LOIS L. KAUFMAN

Comforting Those in Pain

One of the most beautiful personality traits of the Holy Spirit is His ability to comfort His people by lending a helping hand. The book of Acts tells us that the Early Church, though experiencing great persecution, was able to thrive because of the Spirit's presence: "Walking in the fear of the Lord and in the comfort of the Holy Spirit, they were multiplied" (Acts 9:31). If you know someone in pain, lend a hand by pointing them to the Comforter. But don't stop there! Scripture tells us to "comfort those who are in any trouble, with the comfort with which we ourselves are comforted by God" (2 Cor. 1:4). When you think of how God has comforted you in difficult times, you'll know just how to comfort others.

A little girl was late arriving home from school. When she finally arrived, her mother demanded an explanation. The girl explained that on her way home she had spotted a friend crying

Kiss of the sun for pardon.
Song of the birds for mirth.
You're closer to God's heart in a garden
Than any place else on earth.

DOROTHY FRANCES GURNEY

over a broken doll. "Oh," said the mother, "then you stopped to help her fix her doll?"

"Oh, no," the girl replied. "I stopped to help her cry."[2]

Just as a master gardener eagerly shares seed with other gardeners, God spreads the seeds of compassion through His people. Sometimes we simply need to be there for others and show them we care.

Digging Deeper

1. This chapter unearthed three qualities of a master gardener: He or she is hands on, hands off and willing to lend a hand. Fill in the following sentences to uncover the friends who need you to exhibit these qualities:

   _____ needs a hands-on friend. I can help her by . . .

   I could be a little more hands off with _____ because . . .

   My friend _____ needs me to lend a hand with . . .

2. God perfectly displays the attributes of the Master Gardener in the lives of His children. Fill in the following sentences to recount how God has been busy in your life:

   God was very hands on when . . .

I sensed God was being hands off when . . .

God lent a hand by . . .

3. We found that the Holy Spirit is the One who tills the soil in our hearts. Read Romans 5:5 and describe how He does this. How do you think this helps you to be a better friend?

4. Journal a prayer, asking God to pour His love into your heart so that you can pour out His love to your friends.

CHAPTER 3

Roses

Legend has it that many, many years ago, rose bushes had no thorns. One day a deer meandered past a rose in bloom, saw that its petals were beautiful to behold, caught a whiff of its scintillating aroma and took a bite. The deer said, "This is the most delicious flower of all. From now on, I'll only eat roses." Soon the news spread throughout the deer population, and they began to feast on roses for breakfast, lunch and dinner.

The roses were horrified. How could they survive if the deer continued to gobble them up? So the bushes gathered to pray. They called on the Master Gardener, "Please protect us. We'll accept whatever it takes if only You shield us!" The Master Gardener replied, "I'll shield you, but it will cause you some pain." The roses quickly said, "Whatever it takes."

Soon, the roses felt a stabbing sensation in their stems. Something excruciating was happening. After what seemed an eternity, sharp thorns forced their way through the tender green stems of the rose bushes. The roses asked, "How can these painful thorns help us?" "Wait and see," replied the Master.

The next day, the deer sauntered up to feast on the roses. This time, however, when the deer began to nibble, they were pricked by thorns. "Ouch!" said the deer, "maybe roses aren't so tasty after all." And the deer went away to find less thorny eating.

The roses burst forth in a song of gratitude: "Thank You, Master, for our thorns!" So the roses continued to bloom in abundance, sharing their beauty and fragrance with all who passed by.

The rose is known for its four distinct characteristics: (1) splendor, (2) scent, (3) spikes and (4) solitude. Roses are, indeed, beautiful to behold, and their fragrance is beyond compare. But these two pleasant attributes are offset by two less agreeable elements: They bear painful thorns and grow best in private. One rose grower said, "Roses don't like sharing their space. . . . Plants right near the base of a rose make it harder to water and fertilize and may not want the same conditions."[1]

Roses in a garden of friends are easily identified by four similar characteristics. They

- Display great beauty
- Do suffer afflictions
- Discover God's presence in solitude
- Disburse Christ's love

> *God uses broken things. It takes broken soil to produce a crop, broken clouds to give rain, broken grain to give bread, broken bread to give strength. It is the broken alabaster box that gives forth perfume— it is Peter, weeping bitterly, who returns to greater power than ever.*
>
> VANCE HAVNER

You have probably marveled at the women in your life who suffer some type of affliction yet continue to bloom, grow and bestow the perfume of Christ's presence on the lives they touch. I'm sure you've seen how, after spending time alone with the Master Gardener, the roses in your garden of friends have even learned to be thankful for the thorns.

Garden in My Heart

One of the roses I'm privileged to have in my garden is Joni Eareckson Tada. She is well known as a friend to all, especially to those who suffer from disabilities. Her ministry even bears the name *Joni and Friends*.

Displays Great Beauty

Joni is physically beautiful: She has thick blonde hair, an upturned nose, a dazzling smile and an intense gaze. But her outward appearance only hints at the depth of her inward beauty. After learning I had met Joni for lunch, people curiously asked, "What was she like?" I could only say, "She's amazing. I've never met anyone like her."

Joni's beauty has been shaped by affliction. As a teenager, she was paralyzed following a diving accident. Initially, she suffered from despair and hopelessness. However, God revealed Himself to her in the solitude of the hospital room. She doesn't hesitate to remind people that drawing close to Him transformed her life. Joni said, "My wheelchair is the prison God has used to set my spirit free!"

Suffers Afflictions

Joni shares the lessons she has learned from her private pain with people around the world through radio, books, TV and personal appearances. Recently, she brought her message, *The God I Love,* to my hometown of Albuquerque, New Mexico. As the event's coordinator, I watched her go through the dress rehearsal to prepare for the conference. She wheeled onto the stage, positioned her chair exactly in the center and began her run-through. Every now and then I'd see her try to shift positions. She finally told her husband, Ken, "I'm in pain. I think I need an adjustment." I looked at them and said, "Should we stop the rehearsal?" Ken shook his head, *No.* Joni wanted to finish and wouldn't stop until everything was just right. I was worried about Joni and concerned that she wouldn't be able to endure the three-hour conference.

Discovers God's Presence in Solitude

After the rehearsal, Joni went to her dressing room to regroup and spend time alone with the Lord. The committee sponsoring the event gathered to pray as thousands of people, some in wheelchairs, some unable to see, some unable to hear, some broken in spirit and some able-bodied entered the auditorium. Suddenly, I looked up and there was Joni! She cheerfully said, "Is this where we're gathering? I always want to be where there's prayer." I sat amazed at her resilience as she said to the group, "Why don't we sing?" And we did. We sang praise songs and prayed for the Lord's blessing on the evening.

Disburses Christ's Love

No one attending the conference could have perceived that Joni was in pain. She spoke passionately about how God is her strength in weakness. She spoke of the joy of knowing Jesus as Lord and Savior. She interspersed her message with hymns of praise. Untold numbers of people committed their lives to Christ and thousands more were spiritually uplifted by Joni's message of hope.

At the end of her presentation, I thought Joni might need to return to her hotel. Yet there she was in the lobby, signing her books by holding a pen in her mouth, offering smiles and words of encouragement to the people who came to see her. She wouldn't hear of leaving until everyone in line had a chance to meet her. Then she gathered the committee together and prayed, thanking God for His presence and His work among us. It was incredible to see this fragile rose afflicted with the thorn of quadriplegia shower the fragrance of Christ's love upon those with whom she came in contact.

In God's Garden

In God's garden, there are roses who spread spiritual beauty and fragrance. While most of the examples of spiritual flowers in this book are women, Paul the apostle is the best example of a rose in God's garden. His life holds significant lessons for both men and women of faith.

Thorn in the Flesh

In his letter to the Corinthians, Paul wrote that, like a rose, "a thorn in the flesh was given to me" (2 Cor. 12:7). The word "thorn" comes from a Greek word that refers to a stake on which one is impaled.[2] Paul was not specific about the nature of his painful thorn. It could have been a physical infirmity such as epilepsy or bad eyesight. It has been suggested that Paul's thorn was spiritual in nature, relating to the intense persecution from the Jews. Perhaps Paul's thorn was emotional and he experienced the doubts and depression common to all humanity.

While we don't know exactly what Paul's thorn in the flesh was, we can discover three reasons why he experienced it: (1) to put off pride, (2) to promote prayer and (3) to point to God's power.

Put Off Pride

Paul wrote, "Lest I should be exalted above measure by the abundance of the revelations, a thorn in the flesh was given to me, a messenger of Satan to buffet me, lest I be exalted above measure" (2 Cor. 12:7). In other words, God gave Paul many revelations concerning Himself. But He also allowed Paul to experience pain so that he wouldn't take personal pride in what God had revealed. Pride was the sin that caused Satan to rebel against God and it is the sin that can cause believers to feel self-sufficient. Paul's thorn in the flesh kept him ever dependent on God.

Promote Prayer

Another reason Paul endured the thorn in the flesh was to enhance his prayer life. In his letter he said, "Concerning this thing I pleaded with the Lord three times that it might depart from me" (2 Cor. 12:8). Clearly, Paul's affliction caused him to earnestly draw near to God in prayer. Most commentators acknowledge that Paul's prayer life was the secret to his successful ministry. In addition, Paul was never ashamed to ask others to pray for him as he continued in his ministry. Undoubtedly, believer's intercessory prayers on his behalf added to his ministry's fruitfulness.

Point to God's Power

Paul came to understand God's power to use him despite his weakness. Rather than choosing to heal, God sovereignly decided to empower Paul in the midst of his pain. In response to Paul's prayer, God replied, "My grace is sufficient for you, for My strength is made perfect in weakness" (2 Cor. 12:9). Throughout his life, Paul was able to point to God's power as the source of his strength.

God's garden would not be complete without the beauty and the fragrance of the rose. But He graciously allows thorns so that the roses will be humble concerning the work God is doing in their lives, prayerful concerning their pain and dependent upon Him to give them strength.

How Does Your Garden Grow?

If you were to ask me which flower I relate to the best, it would be the rose. In part it's because my married name is Rose. In part it's because I love roses and carried them at my wedding. But mostly, I consider myself a rose because I am called to teach God's Word, sharing the perfume of His grace with other women.

Like other roses, I suffer an affliction. For nearly two decades I've endured migraines. For many years, I had headaches once a week—and each lasted two to three days. Yet God has chosen to use me despite the headaches. For over a decade, He has graciously allowed me to publish Bible studies for women throughout the world and to write study lessons for my home church. He's given me the privilege of traveling and teaching at conferences and retreats. I have learned to rely on God to empower me to participate in the ministry. I realize that nothing in me is able to accomplish God's work. I can say with

> *The coward seeks release from pressure. The courageous pray for strength.*
>
> FRANCES J. ROBERTS

Paul, "I take pleasure in infirmities, in reproaches, in needs, in persecutions, in distresses, for Christ's sake. For when I am weak, then I am strong" (2 Cor. 12:10). I'd probably even say it a little differently: "When I am weak, then *God* is strong." Through the years, God has used my friends to care for me. Let me share three things I've learned through their example in tending roses so that you can help your roses spread the fragrance of Christ to others.

Resist Judging

Some well-intentioned people mistakenly place the blame for all afflictions on sin. They believe that only the sinful will suffer, while the saintly will enjoy perfect health. This could not be further from the truth and is hurtful to those in pain. I've been devastated by people who say, "If you'll only confess your hidden sin, your headaches will disappear." These people have no idea of the hours I've spent in prayer and confession, beseeching God to remove my thorn. You see, while some suffering is the direct result of sin in a believer's life, other suffering is a sign of God's love. The psalmist said, "Many are the afflictions of the righteous" (Ps. 34:19). Sometimes suffering is simply God's way of drawing us nearer to Him. I can honestly say that I have sensed God's presence more in sickness than in health and have even learned to be thankful for the way my thorn has deepened my relationship with Him.

Respect the Need for Solitude

One of God's commands is, "Be still, and know that I am God" (Ps. 46:10). I have to admit that I am by nature a restless creature. If it were not for my headaches, I probably wouldn't be still and listen to what God is telling me. But pain has a way of focusing our attention upward.

I remember one time when my head was aching, a friend of mine came to sit with me. I was in excruciating pain, but I had a deadline for finishing a Bible study that I was writing. My friend kept trying to talk to me, but I couldn't speak. Then she got busy straightening up my room. If you understand migraines, you'll know that even the slightest sound can resonate like a sonic boom when a headache is raging. My friend's every move caused me to wince. Finally, I asked her, "Could you go take Ryan to McDonald's? That would really help." Cheerfully, she bustled out of the house to feed and care for my daughter.

As I lay there in the silence, head throbbing, God began to give me the outline for the lesson I was writing. In that time alone, God spoke to my heart so that I could complete my task. If you have a rose in your life, won't you give her the space and time she needs alone with the Master Gardener?

Resolve to Pray

As Paul revealed in his letter to the Corinthians, his thorn caused him to pray. But many times throughout his letters, he asked his Christian friends to pray for him as well. Prayer is probably the most important means of nurturing your rose.

I'm so honored that a group of my friends prays for me regularly. They pray specifically that God will continue to use me despite my headaches. And their prayers have been answered. Recently, I was teaching a Bible study when a headache hit me like a truck. It was so painful that I thought I was having a stroke. I thought, *How can I continue? I can't even read my notes!* I shot a quick prayer up to God and looked at the front row to my prayer partner, bowing my head to indicate *I need prayer— now!* I saw her lower her head and begin to intercede for me. I can't even remember what I said in that headache-fogged message, but at the end, I gave an altar call and more women than ever before were saved. That was when I clearly understood the power of prayer and the power of God to use the weakest of vessels to accomplish His divine goals.

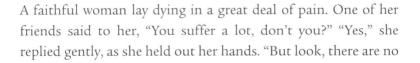

A faithful woman lay dying in a great deal of pain. One of her friends said to her, "You suffer a lot, don't you?" "Yes," she replied gently, as she held out her hands. "But look, there are no nails here. He had the nails; I have the peace!" Then she put her hand on her brow and said, "See, there are no thorns here. He had the thorns, I have the peace!"[3]

The thorns Christ wore on the cross were more painful than anything we could endure, because they were the thorns of all humankind, the thorns that purchased our peace. If you are a rose, take the time to thank God for the thorns you bear, and especially give thanks for the thorns He allowed His Son to wear.

Digging Deeper

1. Describe the friend in your garden who is most like a rose. How have you seen her grow spiritually through painful circumstances?

2. We saw that Paul's affliction alleviated pride, promoted prayer and pointed to God's power. Take a look at Psalm 119:67; then describe another way affliction brings us closer to God. Why do you think this is so?

3. Journal about an affliction you face. Describe how it has humbled you and caused you to be still and know that He is God.

4. One mistake some people make is judging people by assuming their suffering is the result of sin. Read the following Scriptures and explain what the Bible teaches about judging others.

    Matthew 7:1-2

    1 Corinthians 4:4-5

5. How will you help the rose in your life to bloom and disperse the scent of her Savior?

    ❒ Pray for her regularly
    ❒ Pay attention to her insights
    ❒ Provide a quiet time without distraction
    ❒ Other _____

CHAPTER 4
Lilies

Many non-Christian religions mandate that their followers saturate their minds with the sacred writings of their faith. For instance, no one can teach in an Islamic mosque until he has memorized the entire Koran. One missionary tells of how she listened to a group of Buddhist priests quote their devotional literature from memory—for 21 hours nonstop. They rarely, if ever, made a mistake. Sadly, many Christians don't follow the same spiritual discipline of regularly meditating on and memorizing the true Word of God.

However, in some people's lives, God's Word is taken to heart. Michael Billester once gave a Bible to a villager in eastern Poland. Returning a few years later, he learned that 200 people had become believers as a result of having read this single Bible. When the group gathered to hear him preach, he suggested that before he spoke each person should quote his or her favorite Scriptures. One man rose and asked, "Perhaps, Brother, we've misunderstood you. Did you mean verses or chapters?" Billester was astonished. "Are you saying there are people here who can recite complete chapters of the Bible?" That was precisely the case. In fact, 13 of the villagers had memorized half of Genesis as well as the books of Matthew and Luke. Another person had committed the Psalms to memory. Combined, the 200 villagers knew practically the entire Bible.[1] These Polish villagers can be regarded as spiritual lilies.

Lilies are statuesque flowers, standing tall and drawing admiration for their trumpet-like silhouette and exquisite scent. Their distinct blossom resembles a stunning six-petaled star.

Generally, lilies are raised from bulbs. The bulbs function as food reserves, enabling the plants to be self-feeding. The lilies in our friendship garden, then, are those who devotedly feed on God's Word to maintain their spiritual growth. The Hebrew name for lily is *shushan*, which means "whiteness."[2] Thus, the lily symbolizes a pure and holy life. Since they are capable of nurturing themselves and have a long blooming season, most gardeners consider lilies to be very reliable. Spiritual lilies exhibit the same faithful qualities, desiring purity and proving themselves true to their friends and their God.

The lily is also extremely prolific. Since one root yields many bulbs, lilies have the capacity for self-multiplication. At my house, one lily planted a decade ago has multiplied into countless lilies adorning our yard. We've even dug up the bulbs, divided them and planted them in many barren areas on our property. Spiritually, a lily will be fruitful, helping to multiply God's family by exemplifying a faithful life and dispersing her knowledge of God's Word to others.

Like the lilies in the earth's garden, you can recognize the lilies in your garden of friends by three outstanding characteristics. They are

- Faithful to God's ways
- Self-fed by God's Word
- Fruitful as God's witnesses

The lily is a perfect picture of spiritual vitality. By feeding on God's Word, our lily friends grow faithful in God's ways. This faithfulness leads to fruitful witnessing of God's love and power to save. The lily is so attractive because she both beautifies and expands the kingdom of God on Earth.

The Garden in My Heart

The first lily I ever knew was my grandmother, Lillian. Though she was my grandmother, I also considered her one of my dearest friends. She listened to my secrets without judging, she laughed at my jokes, she loved me unconditionally, and she always pointed me to Christ.

Faithful to God's Ways

Mima's name, Lillian, derived from the word "lily," fit her so well. She was a woman who was truly pure in heart. I never heard her say a bad thing about anyone, even the people who came into her store with complaints or excuses for not paying their bills. And she loved God's Word. Without fail, whenever I'd visit her, I would find her reading her Bible before bedtime and praying. She'd look up with her gentle doe-brown eyes and murmur, "This way I know I'll get a good night's rest."

I was a college student when she was diagnosed with cancer. Yet even as she lay dying, she continued reading Scripture and praying for her children and grandchildren on a daily basis. I know she prayed especially hard for me, because in high school I had walked away from the Lord and had begun to walk in the ways of the world. The night before she died, I sat in my grandmother's room reading a magazine. Suddenly, she looked up at someone in the room whom I couldn't see. A serene smile transformed her pain-wracked face, her eyes lit up, and she nodded her head as if to say, "I'm ready to go—transplant me to heaven."

One of my deepest regrets is that my grandmother didn't live to see me recommit my life to Christ. It's been said that God doesn't have grandchildren, only children; but largely because of the prayers and example of my lily-like grandmother and the other lilies I know, I am now firmly planted in God's garden.

It's been over 20 years since her death, but the impact of my grandmother's faith has resonated throughout our entire family. Today, her children, grandchildren and great-grandchildren are all followers of Christ. What an amazingly fruitful legacy she left behind!

> *We can never be lilies in the garden unless we have spent time as bulbs in the dark, totally ignored.*
>
> OSWALD CHAMBERS

Self-fed on God's Word

My friend and spiritual mentor, Lenya Heitzig, also exhibits the qualities of a lily. I can't count the number of times I've called her in the morning and asked, "Whatcha doin'?" So often her reply is, "Having morning devotionals." She takes a book bag with a Bible, a notebook, a pen and a devotional with her wherever she goes. She calls it her "lunch bag" because it carries her spiritual food. Wherever she goes, she can "eat" of God's Word. Like the psalmist, she loves to "taste and see that the LORD is good" (Ps. 34:8).

A few years ago, I accompanied her on a retreat at which she was speaking, and I listened in on some of her conversations. She was constantly quoting the Bible as she counseled and comforted the women she met. The retreat planner said to me, "I think if you cut her, she'd bleed Scripture." It's true—most of her conversation is laced with biblical insights and references.

Fruitful as God's Witness

Lenya and her husband, Pastor Skip Heitzig, founded Calvary of Albuquerque, a church with a humble beginning. It began as a small Bible study in an apartment building soon after the Heitzigs were married. Because they were faithful to plant God's Word, the church grew from 9 attendees to over 14,000 people today. The women's ministry experienced similar growth, beginning with a handful of ladies and burgeoning to over 1,000 Bible students.

But faithfulness and fruitfulness can be costly. Recently, Lenya and Skip felt the Lord's call to transplant them to a new field. Just as lilies are multiplied by dividing their roots, the Heitzigs felt the Lord's call to multiply their ministry by beginning a new one. Though it was difficult for me to watch them go, since then I've seen God use them in amazing ways in their new territory.

If you were to ask me the key lesson I've learned from my lily friend, Lenya, I would repeat one of her favorite sayings: "The Word of God does the work of God." By faithfully staying in God's Word and seeking God's will, Lenya has drawn thousands of women, including me, to a closer relationship with Christ.

The lilies in my garden of friends have planted a desire in my heart to become more like them: to immerse myself in God's Word, to obey what I read, to tell others what I've learned. By mirroring their godly habits, we can all come to look like lilies in God's field of flowers.

In God's Garden

One of the lilies in God's garden was Priscilla. She and her husband, Aquila, were early converts to the Christian faith. Paul commended Priscilla and Aquila as "fellow workers in Christ Jesus" (Rom. 16:3).

Deep-Rooted Faith

Like Paul, Priscilla and Aquila were tentmakers. Paul lived with the couple and taught them the foundations of the faith as "he reasoned in the synagogue every Sabbath, and persuaded both Jews and Greeks" (Acts 18:4). Paul stayed in Corinth "a year and six months, teaching the word of God among them" (Acts 18:11).

Scripture is clear that Priscilla and Aquila fed on God's Word, and the truths took root deep in their hearts. But they didn't just feed on Scripture; they also fed others in the faith. They journeyed with Paul to Ephesus and started a thriving church in their home, sharing biblical truths they had learned as they opened their door to spiritual seekers (see Acts 18:18).

Fervent Faith

This godly couple clearly loved God's Word and had a fervent desire that it be represented with accuracy. Priscilla and Aquila took the time to help a man named Apollos grow in the knowledge of the Lord. It seems that Apollos was an extremely charismatic speaker and fervent in the faith. But after hearing him teach, Priscilla and Aquila realized Apollos didn't have a complete understanding of God's Word. They realized that Apollos couldn't teach others without a deeper understanding of Scripture. The book of Acts tells us that "when Aquila and Priscilla heard him, they took him aside and explained to him the way of God more accurately" (Acts 18:26). With his new spiritual insight, Apollos became an even more powerful teacher, helping to expand the Early Church by coming alongside Paul and nurturing converts to Christianity (see vv. 27-28).

Spreading Faith

As a lily, Priscilla consumed a steady diet of God's Word and was faithful to share it with those she met. At great risk to herself, she willingly opened her home to spread the gospel message to those in her community who were hungry for the truth. Not only did she minister to those in her sphere of influence but she also was fruitful through her mentorship of Apollos, who went on to spread the gospel message in distant lands, "showing from the Scriptures that Jesus is the Christ" (Acts 18:28). Truly, through Priscilla's influence, the gospel message spread far and wide.

The best way for Christians to grow is to eat the Bread of Life.

ANONYMOUS

As you think about God's garden, follow Jesus' advice to "consider the lilies" (Luke 12:27). Lilies are not only beautiful but they also spread rapidly because they can nurture and sustain themselves. Ask God to make you a lily in His garden, constantly feeding on the Word of God and sharing your faith with others so the kingdom of God can expand.

How Does Your Garden Grow?

I believe that God plants lilies in our lives because He knows we need friends that we can count on—beautiful and hardy souls, friends who encourage us to maintain a steady diet of Scripture so that we can multiply His love.

Here are three helpful tips to help you foster the growth of the lilies in your garden of friends.

Encourage Them

Because they have a deep knowledge of God's Word, lilies should be encouraged to share what they know with others rather than keeping it to themselves. As part of the Great Commission, Jesus told His disciples to "go therefore and make disciples of all the nations . . . teaching them to observe all things that I have commanded you" (Matt. 28:19-20). One of the greatest responsibilities of acquiring spiritual knowledge is to dispense it to others. I'm not saying that all lilies have to be like Lenya—Bible study teachers who speak to hundreds of women. Like my grandmother, lilies can have just as profound an impact ministering one-on-one to their friends, family and coworkers.

One lily aficionado wrote, "Lilies MUST HAVE GOOD DRAINAGE!!! It is rule No. 1 for success with lilies . . . also Rule No. 2, No. 3, No. 4 and No. 5! If you are going to choose a spot where water collects and stands, you might as well take your hard-earned dollar bills out and plant them instead . . . you will have about as much chance of raising a crop!"[3]

Like the flower, our lily friends need drainage to remain spiritually vivacious—they need to pour out what they know. This need is best illustrated by the two seas in Israel. One, the Sea of Galilee, is fresh and fruitful. The other, the Dead Sea, is desolate and virtually lifeless. What's the difference? While both are fed by the Jordan River, the Sea of Galilee has drainage, pouring itself out onto the fertile Jordan River plain. On the other hand, the Dead Sea only collects water without channeling it anywhere, rendering the Dead Sea useless and unhealthy. Be sure to encourage the lilies you know to become like the Sea of Galilee. Help them to become conduits for scriptural knowledge so that they don't grow stagnant and stale.

Enhance Them

A lily expert tells us to put "mulch around the stems . . . or a ground cover . . . [to] hold the soil and keep it from washing away."[4] In other words, lilies need protection. We can enhance our lilies' lives by covering them so that they are free to study God's Word.

Remember how the Early Church was taxing the disciples' energy for Bible study, washing away their time in the Word by expecting them to wait on tables? The disciples said,

> It is not desirable that we should leave the word of God and serve tables. Therefore, brethren, seek out from among you seven men of good reputation, full of the Holy Spirit and wisdom, whom we may appoint over this business; but we will give ourselves continually to prayer and to the ministry of the word (Acts 6:2-4).

If you are a woman "of good reputation, full of the Holy Spirit and wisdom," you'll notice when others are asking too much of the lilies. That's when you can step in and do some of the work they needn't be doing. Perhaps a lily in your life needs you to come alongside her with your gift of administration to help keep her paperwork in order. Maybe she needs your gift of helps to take care of her children while she's studying. It could be she needs your gift of hospitality to cook a meal for her family while she prepares a spiritual meal. You can enhance your lily's life by covering for her, so she can study the Word and minister to others. As a pastor's wife, Lenya has often said, "I want to do the work that only I can do, and equip others to do the work that only they can do."

Emulate Them

As I was studying the lily to write this chapter, I kept thinking, *I want to be like a lily*. I believe we can all be various flowers at various times. If we want to become like a lily, we need to emulate their habits. Our transformation may not happen immediately, but if we follow the ways of the lily, we'll begin to take on the characteristics of the lily. It's really a simple process: When we feed on the Word, we will become faithful; when we act faithfully, we will be fruitful. We can follow Paul's advice: "The things which you learned and received and heard and saw in me, these do, and the God of peace will be with you" (Phil. 4:9).

The story is told about the time a rabbinic student quoted Old Testament Scripture to his teacher: "These commandments that I give you today are to be upon your hearts" (Deut. 6:6, *NIV*). He then asked, "Why are we told to place God's Word *upon* rather than *in* our heart?" The rabbi answered that he did not believe it is within man's power to place the divine teachings directly in his heart. "All we can do is place God's Word on the surface of our heart so that when the heart breaks they will drop in."[5] Won't you allow the truth of God's Word to break your heart so that it can penetrate deep within and bring you to spiritual maturity? Then you, too, can be a beautiful lily in God's garden.

Digging Deeper

1. Name the friend(s) you consider to be a lily in your Garden of Friends, and describe how she exhibits the lily's characteristics.

2. Think about and then share some of the ways you will encourage, enhance or emulate your lily.

3. We've discovered that one of the key attributes of the lily is that she "feeds" on God's Word. Fill in the chart on the next page to discover some benefits of spending time in Scripture.

Scripture	Benefits of God's Word
Psalm 119:9	
Psalm 119:11	
Psalm 119:28	
Psalm 119:50	
Psalm 119:105	

4. Journal about how you have personally benefited from spending time in God's Word.

5. Rewrite Psalm 119:103-4 into a personal prayer, asking God to give you a taste for His Word so that you can receive His wisdom and guidance:

How sweet are Your words to my taste,
sweeter than honey to my mouth!
Through Your precepts I get understanding;
therefore I hate every false way (Ps. 119:103-4).

CHAPTER 5

Violets

In the Land of Long Ago and Far Away, winter and summer were the only two seasons. The ruler of the realm, King Weather, grew lonely in his solitary palace, so he sent out courtiers in search of a lovely girl to bring him happiness. The courtiers found many beautiful women, but alas, they were either too cold in feeling or too hot in temperament. The search continued until one day the king's men happened upon a shy maiden standing in the shadows of her father's castle. Her name was Violet. The courtiers described King Weather's predicament to her. Violet's heart went out to the lonely king, and she agreed to meet him. Though it was winter and she was withering in the cold, the king saw Violet's vibrant beauty, sensed her sweet spirit and fell deeply in love with her. She loved him in return, but his castle was too frosty in winter and too sizzling in summer for her to survive.

Violet evaluated the situation and came up with a plan, "Oh, dear king, gladly would I dwell with you, but you must protect me from the elements." The king saw the wisdom of her request and immediately called for the master builders to erect a conservatory where his bride, Violet, could pass the icy winter months and hot summer days. And so it came to pass that Violet lived in the castle where her love transformed the lonesome king.

Such was the tender effect of Violet upon her husband that he decreed, "In this realm, we shall have two new seasons, springtime and fall. From this time forward, winter and summer shall only occupy half the year." Thus, whenever the climate was mild, Violet emerged to spread joy and kindness throughout the land.[1]

The phrase most commonly associated with the violet is "shrinking violet," but it is also celebrated as a "sweet violet." A delicate flower, it wilts in extreme temperatures, breaks in the wind and bruises if treated roughly. Violets tend to grow in springtime and autumn when the climate is temperate but wilt when the heat is on and shrivel in the cold. They grow best in the gentle morning sun or shaded areas and need to be protected from the wind. But when violets are nurtured in suitable conditions, they are sweet scented and full of vibrant color. The lovely flower has such a distinct shade that one of Crayola's first crayons, introduced in 1903, was called Violet.

Don't you have friends like the violet? Ladies who don't like to take center stage but prefer to stay in the shadows? We all know violets, or have been violets, bruised and brokenhearted by the winds of life. Yet violets can flourish and extend their influence over a large area, making the world a lovelier place to live.

Our violet friends share characteristics similar to those of the tender purple flower. They

- Shun the limelight
- Spread vibrant color
- Stoop over

Down in a green and shady bed,
 A modest violet grew;
Its stalk was bent, it hung its head
 As if to hide from view.
And yet it was a lovely flow'r,
 Its colors bright and fair,
It might have graced a rosy bow'r
 Instead of hiding there.

Yet there it was content to bloom,
 In modest tints arrayed;
And there it spread its sweet perfume
 Within the silent shade,
Then let me to the valley go,
 This pretty flow'r to see,
That I may also learn to grow
 In sweet humility.

JANE TAYLOR 1783-1824

I'm grateful for the violets in my life who, with humility and tenderness, spread the color of God's love.

The Garden in My Heart

I look at my friend Christy as a sweet violet. I've known Christy and her family since elementary school. In the early days, she wasn't actually my friend, she was my friend Lori's cool older sister.

Shuns the Limelight

When I was a freshman in high school, Christy was a senior varsity cheerleader. I wanted to be just like her. She was cute, kind and popular. Some of the cheerleaders were flamboyant, always drawing attention to themselves; but Christy was different. She didn't mind being the "base" in the stunts so that others could climb high. She'd stand back and grin when her more showy teammates grabbed the spotlight. She was clearly more comfortable playing a supporting role than being the star.

When we grew up, Christy and I began to attend the same church. Over time, we developed our own friendship. She was no longer just Lori's big sister to be admired; she was my friend. I was surprised to discover that Christy was really shy. She spoke in soft tones and seemed slightly uncomfortable when attention was focused on her. Like a violet at ease in the shadows, Christy blossoms when the limelight is on others. Perhaps the best word to describe this is "humility." Christy exhibits the humble heart extolled in Scripture: "Let nothing be done through selfish ambition or conceit, but in lowliness of mind let each esteem others better than himself" (Phil. 2:3).

Spreads Vibrant Color

Every garden needs a hint of purple. One gardening expert wrote,

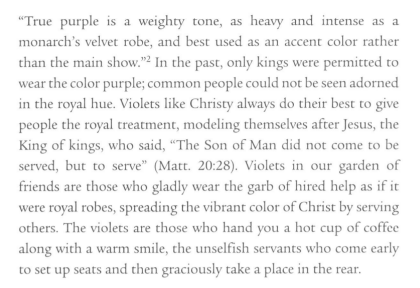

"True purple is a weighty tone, as heavy and intense as a monarch's velvet robe, and best used as an accent color rather than the main show."[2] In the past, only kings were permitted to wear the color purple; common people could not be seen adorned in the royal hue. Violets like Christy always do their best to give people the royal treatment, modeling themselves after Jesus, the King of kings, who said, "The Son of Man did not come to be served, but to serve" (Matt. 20:28). Violets in our garden of friends are those who gladly wear the garb of hired help as if it were royal robes, spreading the vibrant color of Christ by serving others. The violets are those who hand you a hot cup of coffee along with a warm smile, the unselfish servants who come early to set up seats and then graciously take a place in the rear.

Stoops Over

Violets not only shun the limelight and spread the royal color but they also stoop over. The violet grows from a single stalk and boasts five heart-shaped petals on each flower. The flower seems to hang its head in sorrow. So, too, our violet friends prove to be exceptionally sympathetic, feeling the pain of their friends and longing to comfort them.

Many times I've watched Christy lean into a friend, listening to her problems and weeping over her pain. Her nonthreatening posture welcomes confidences as she bends over to comfort and console others. Our violet friends are those who freely "rejoice with those who rejoice, and weep with those who weep" (Rom. 12:15).

Oh, that we could all be more like the violet—that we would graciously step back in support of others; that we would display the King of king's royal color by humbly serving those in need; that we would follow the biblical mandate "to comfort those who are in any trouble, with the comfort with which we ourselves are comforted by God" (2 Cor 1:4).

In God's Garden

There are many violets growing in the shade of God's garden. Perhaps the woman most associated with the royal color is Lydia, "a seller of purple" (Acts 16:14). Scripture reveals how this remarkable woman exhibited the attributes of a sweet violet: a humble heart, a servant's stance and a sympathetic spirit.

Going Low

To be humble means to lie low, to recognize that all we are or have comes from God. Humility is freedom from arrogance and is characterized by dependence on God as well as the exaltation of others above self.[3] The first time we encounter Lydia in the Bible, she was humbling herself before God beside the river "where prayer was customarily made" (Acts 16:13). Lydia was a Gentile proselyte who had come to believe in the Jewish God. She was known as one who "worshiped God" (v. 14). And Lydia was humble enough to recognize her need for a Savior. Scripture tells how her humble devotion to God led her to saving faith: "The Lord opened her heart to heed the things spoken by Paul" (v. 14). Lydia's ability to go low allowed her to discover the God most high.

Role Reversal

We learn that following her conversion, Lydia was selfless, even toward her servants. She made sure the members of "her household were baptized" (Acts 16:15). This was truly remarkable, for in those days servants were considered property to be bought and sold, not people to be cared for and loved. Lydia exhibited the first and greatest act of humility by turning her heart, mind and soul over to the Lord. From this, she grew in humility, selflessly serving others—even her own servants.

In the Bible, there were different types of servants. A servant could be a slave under the command of a master, a person hired to complete tasks with the liberty to take or leave a job, or a volunteer freely choosing to do another's bidding.[4] Of her own free will, Lydia worked to show herself a faithful servant of her heavenly Master. Though a prosperous businesswoman, Lydia was not ashamed to take a servant's stance by inviting the apostles into her home. Luke recalls how "she begged us, saying, 'If you have judged me to be faithful to the Lord, come to my house and stay'" (Acts 16:15). By volunteering her home to the missionary team, Lydia displayed the gift of hospitality, opening her home for use as a church. Just think of the behind-the-scenes work involved in preparing a place week after week for services: cleaning, setting up, tearing down and starting all over again. Lydia was willing to work hard behind the scenes so that others would come to know Christ.

Bending Over Backwards

Not surprisingly, the name "Lydia" means "bending."[5] I'm sure her name matched her character. Like a violet, she bent down in support and sympathy to those in need. For instance, the Jews in Philippi accused Paul and Silas of unlawful conduct. The apostles were beaten with rods and thrown into prison (see Acts 16:22-23). In jail, they experienced "a great earthquake, so that the foundations of the prison were shaken" (v. 26). Following their release, the men "went out of the prison and entered the house of Lydia" (v. 40). It's easy to understand that following such a great ordeal, the ill-treated men would seek a safe and nurturing environment. Lydia offered the perfect respite for the men, personally living out Paul's instructions: "Let each of you look out not only for his own interests, but also for the interests of others" (Phil. 2:4). In essence, Lydia bent over backwards, even putting her household at risk, to help her beloved brethren.

We see in Lydia and the lives of our violet-like friends how the violet is truly a royal flower, displaying the characteristics of a true daughter of the King of kings: humble in heart, selfless in service and sympathetic in spirit.

How Does Your Garden Grow?

Violets bloom best under temperate conditions with just the right amount of attention. When treated properly, they will flourish in a garden, adding color in the dark corners. Our friends who resemble the violet add vibrant color to our lives. To help our violet friends grow and blossom, we can help cultivate them properly by not "over" or "under" doing it. I've learned that we shouldn't overlook, underlight, or overload our violet friends. In addition, we should learn from our violets to avoid overcommitting.

Don't Overlook

One violet grower cautions against neglecting violets. She says, "They need some attention just as you do to thrive. They should be rotated weekly so that the light is evenly directed to all sides of the plant. If never rotated, the plant will grow lopsided."[6] It's easy to take our violet friends for granted, because they are not attention hounds, preferring the spotlight to stay off them. But they do need consistent, soft light to grow.

Scripture speaks of the light emitted from Spirit-filled people. When Daniel was brought before the king, his reputation for radiating God's light went before him. The king said, "I have heard of you, that the Spirit of God is in you, and that light and understanding and excellent wisdom are found in you" (Dan. 5:14). As a believer, you can shine the gentle light of understanding and wisdom upon your violet friends.

Don't Underlight

Oftentimes, we fail to shine the light of appreciation on our violet friends. They are so humble and self-effacing that we forget to praise them for their participation in our lives. A simple "thank you" will brighten the hearts of a violet for many days.

In addition, we sometimes fail to ensure that our violets receive balanced light. Scripture reveals that God's Word is "a light that shines in a dark place" (2 Pet. 1:19). You see, violets are so focused on others that they have a tendency to grow spiritually lopsided. You can help by "rotating" their focus, ensuring that good works don't take the place of godly worship. Remind your violets that acts of service must be balanced with the light of God's Word so that they can grow upright.

Don't Overload

Most experts caution against planting violets too close together. They should be planted in deep soil approximately one foot apart. Sometimes, violets produce nothing but leaves. One botanist addressed this problem, saying, "The plants may have been healthy enough to begin with and they were probably well and truly planted, but after the first season of bloom they were allowed to spread and become overcrowded."[7]

Oftentimes we make the same mistake with our violet friends. We overload them and let them spread themselves too thin. Since violets are so eager to help, they have a hard time saying no. I've been guilty of this in my relationship with Christy. When I'm organizing an event, she is one of the first people I call. However, others call on her, too: her daughter's soccer team, the youth group, her friends and her family. There have been times when she has been slightly overwhelmed. If your violet friends are overloaded, ease their burden by releasing them from responsibilities or helping them with their commitments.

Don't Overcommit

As women, it's easy to fall into the trap of agreeing to do far too much. Several years ago, as a young mother of three small children and busy with women's ministry, I said yes to far too many things and got overloaded. Eventually my husband, Kerry, and I sat down to have a heart-to-heart talk. He wisely reminded me that "no" is a spiritual word. He said, "Remember that Jesus said, 'Let your "Yes" be "Yes," and your "No," "No."' Why don't you say no to some things, Penny?"

I know it's flattering to be sought after for help. As women, we may even feel guilty if we turn someone down. But I learned a valuable lesson from a violet named Amy. She said, "I've discovered that every need is not a call. I pray and ask God if He is calling me before I agree to participate. If I'm not the one He's called, He'll provide just the right person."

If you have a violet friend who tends to overcommit herself, remind her that it's OK to say no. In fact, it's biblical.

***

Most of us think of the rose as the Valentine's Day flower. But it's time to set the record straight: The violet is the true flower for Valentines.

Valentine's Day began in honor of a Christian priest named Valentine who was known for his good works. When a cruel Roman emperor heard of him, he threw the priest in prison. According to the legend, Valentine saw the purple flowers growing in the shade of the prison. He gathered the flowers growing outside his cell and crushed the violet's blossoms to make ink. Using the precious purple ink, he wrote encouraging notes to his flock. It is said that Valentine even wrote on a daily basis to his jailer's blind daughter and miraculously cured her ailment.

Since that time, the violet has been the symbol of faithfulness and love.[8] So even if it's not Valentine's Day, won't you let your violets know how much you love and appreciate them?

Digging Deeper

1. As you were reading about the violet, which of your friends came to mind? Write about how she displays the characteristics of this flower in the garden in your heart.

2. Perhaps the loveliest characteristic of the violet is her humility. Read 1 Peter 5:5-7 and explain the spiritual benefits of being "clothed with humility" (v. 5).

3. Journal about a time when, like the violet, you were overloaded with responsibilities.

4. Read Matthew 11:28-30 and answer the following questions:

What encouragement do you receive from the words of Jesus?

What burden is overwhelming you right now?

Write a prayer, laying your burden upon the strong shoulders of your Lord.

Geraniums

We all love stories of individuals who have overcome impossible odds. We delight when the turtle wins the race against the hare; when Roadrunner outfoxes Wile E. Coyote; and when Cinderella marries Prince Charming despite so many obstacles, including her evil stepmother, working against her. There's just something about overcoming adversity that appeals to the human spirit.

Perhaps the pop culture icon that best exemplifies this is the Timex wristwatch. Remember John Cameron Swayze's "torture test" commercials involving the Timex in the late 1950s? The marketing campaign was so popular that by the end of the decade, one out of every three watches bought in the United States was a Timex.[1] Americans watched in fascination as a Timex watch was taped to the propeller of an outboard motor, tumbled over the Grand Coulee Dam or attached to a diver leaping from the cliffs of Acapulco to the sea, 87 feet below. We couldn't imagine that a puny wristwatch could survive these extreme conditions, but somehow it did. The phrase that captured the personality of the plucky Timex watch became a credo to live by: "It takes a licking and keeps on ticking."

In the flower world, the hardy geranium is one of the most popular summer annuals because it can be planted during the heat of the summer and bloom continuously when the temperature spikes upward. Geraniums adorn gardens and patios in the warmest regions of the world, from Israel and Greece to sunny California. Often they are planted in pots so that their clustered, vibrant beauty can adorn bland tile and concrete patios. Geraniums flourish when their dead or fading clusters are pinched off to promote fuller growth. They are showy, bright colored flowers whose beauty makes the summer heat tolerable.

In terms of friends, I consider geraniums to be the Timex of friends. A geranium friend is the Roadrunner who looks into the screen and with a grin says, "Beep beep!" even after an anvil weighing thousands of pounds has crashed down upon her. She is the slow but steady tortoise who keeps on keeping on despite impossible odds; she is the dowdy Cinderella transformed into a princess, winning the heart of the prince. Geraniums are the friends who have experienced the hottest heat of life's trials yet somehow bloom brightly.

I'm sure you have geranium friends who take the heat, keep on blooming and make life beautiful. Their characteristics are easy to recognize. They

- Are able to stand alone
- Are able to withstand heat
- Understand the pinch of pain

I believe that God planted geraniums in my garden of friends to remind me that no matter how hot the circumstances become, beauty can thrive. I've found strength knowing that if my geranium friends can "take a licking and keep on ticking," then, with God's help, so can I.

The Garden in My Heart

My mother, Janelle, displays many characteristics of the geranium. She is a bright, dependable flower blooming in my heart's garden. I've watched her endure seasons of incredible heat: caring for a dying mother, making decisions for a father with dementia and enduring the death of a grandchild. I've often heard her say, "What doesn't kill you only makes you stronger." Over the years, she has continued to grow strong, always pointing her family and friends to God, the source of her strength.

Stands Alone

Several years ago, I met a gal named Katherine who, like my mom, is a sturdy and colorful geranium. Though Katherine is short in stature, she's a dynamo in personality. Her vibrancy drew me to her, and we became fast friends. As I learned the story of Katherine's life, I was amazed at how the hardships she had endured had shaped her into the godly woman she is today. I look at her as a bright red geranium—she is a strong, sturdy and sensational flower in my garden of friends.

Geraniums, rather than being planted in a bed full of other flowers, often find their homes in singular pots. Like a geranium, Katherine learned early in adulthood to stand alone. She was married with two small children when things at home began to fall apart. Following a painful divorce, Katherine took on the role of single motherhood and all of the tireless responsibilities that go along with it. When she reached the end of her rope, she reached out to God to save her. After turning her life over to Christ, Katherine learned that God would be a husband to her and a father to her children. She began to live the Scripture "Now she who is . . . left alone, trusts in God and continues in supplications and prayers night and day" (1 Tim. 5:5). Katherine discovered that standing alone physically doesn't necessarily mean walking alone spiritually.

Withstands Heat

Geraniums can also withstand heat. They don't need much shade and do best when the sun shines on them at least six hours a day. I've seen in Katherine's life the amazing ability to handle incessantly hot situations that would make anyone else wilt or wither.

Several years after coming to Christ, Katherine married a godly man and they had a son together. They began to blend as a family when she was faced with one of the most heated situations a parent can face: a wayward child. Though she had raised her oldest daughter with godly values, the teenaged Laurel turned prodigal. She started by ditching school and then experimented with drugs and alcohol. She began to hang out with a dangerous crowd, and ultimately, she completely rebelled against her mother's authority. Things got so bad that Laurel eventually stooped to stealing from her mom and later to running away from home. The family endured the heat of heartbreak over a straying family member, but Katherine stayed spiritually strong despite the fiery trial.

> *God uses Christians who stay cool in hot places, sweet in sour places, and little in big places.*
>
> ANONYMOUS

At one point, when Katherine realized that Laurel had stolen her car, she began to pray, "Lord, give me wisdom," and then bravely called the police and turned her errant (unlicensed) daughter in to the authorities. When Laurel was apprehended, Katherine did one of the most difficult things a parent can do: She let her child experience the consequences for her actions. With every emotion telling her to rescue her daughter and shield her from facing a penalty, Katherine made the tough decision to press charges and let her child experience the juvenile justice system. She recognized that Laurel's behavior was affecting the younger children in the family and that her influence in the home had become so dangerous and disruptive that she needed to be set apart from the others so that she could be set right.

Understands Pain

A geranium requires that any fading or weak branches be pinched off so that the plant can grow back stronger, with more flower blooms. Katherine realized that this was what Laurel needed—to be removed from the household so that she could get the help she needed. The greatest pain Katherine has ever experienced was allowing her daughter to be sent to a facility for wayward teens. But this story has a happy ending. At the teen home, Laurel accepted Jesus as Lord. Joyfully, Katherine drove to the small mountain town that housed the youth facility and saw her daughter baptized into God's kingdom.

Though others had advised against it, Katherine made a tough decision for her entire family's well-being. With God's help, she was able to withstand the heat of raising a prodigal child. Despite the pain, she learned an important spiritual principle that all parents need to know: Sometimes you have to let children go to help them grow.

In God's Garden

I look at Timothy's godly mother, Eunice, as a geranium in God's garden. Though more is written about her son than is written about her, several passages in the New Testament allow us to catch glimpses into Eunice's life. We see her ability to stand alone; we see that through faith she could withstand the heat of difficult circumstances; and we appreciate that she understood the pain of separation.

Unequally Yoked

We first meet Eunice in the book of Acts when Paul and Silas arrive in her hometown of Lystra. The Bible describes her as "a certain Jewish woman who believed" (Acts 16:1). However, this believing woman was married to an unbelieving husband. Scripture tells us that Timothy's "father was Greek" (Acts 16:1). These insights into Timothy's home life also hint at Eunice's ability to stand alone, raising her son in the faith despite her husband's unbelief.

Only those of you who live with an unbelieving spouse can comprehend the difficulties of training a child in a Christian manner without the support of your husband. Let's face it, raising children when parents agree on a Christian worldview is difficult enough, but raising them when the parents have different value systems makes a tough job much tougher. Fortunately, though Eunice stood alone in her faith when it came to her marriage, she was supported in her faith by her mother, Lois. Isn't that so typical of our gracious God—helping us when we feel alone? Many times He'll send others to stand beside us and support us.

Doubtless, Eunice had to learn to withstand the heat of difficult circumstances. Surely her husband was less than supportive of her faith. I've noticed that many unbelieving husbands try to draw their Christian wives into their sinful lifestyles. Perhaps they do this because their wife's example has begun to prick their consciences and they want to alleviate personal guilt. Often, they are opposed to Christianity but are familiar enough with Christian lingo to order their wives to "submit" to unrighteous acts. But there is no indication in Scripture that Eunice was tempted to act like the pagan Greeks. Her name means "good victory," and Scripture confirms that she was victorious in her personal faith and in nurturing her son's faith. Paul commended Eunice's impact on Timothy, saying, "I call to remembrance the genuine faith that is in you, which dwelt first in your grandmother Lois and your mother Eunice" (2 Tim. 1:5). Eunice's faith was strong enough to withstand the pressure at home.

Culture Clash

In addition, Eunice's faith must have been strong enough to withstand the heat of superstition and persecution outside the home. Lystra, her hometown, was located in Asia Minor. It was known as a wild place with a crude population.[2] The people were highly superstitious, believing that Paul was the god Zeus after he healed a lame man. They even tried to offer sacrifices to Paul. And they were also, unfortunately, easily influenced. They quickly turned against Paul when Jews from Antioch and Iconium came to town and "persuaded the multitudes" (Acts 14:19). The people became so hostile that "they stoned Paul and dragged him out of the city, supposing him to be dead" (v. 19). This was the atmosphere in which Eunice lived: a town eager to embrace idolatry and just as eager to persecute Christianity. No doubt Eunice herself experienced persecution. Paul told Timothy, "All who desire to live godly in Christ Jesus will suffer persecution" (2 Tim. 3:12). The believers in Lystra were certainly no exception. Yet Eunice stood strong against the loose standards of her environment, never wavering in her beliefs, and faithfully teaching the Word of God to her son. As Paul said to Timothy, she made sure "that from childhood you have known the Holy Scriptures, which are able to make you wise for salvation through faith which is in Christ Jesus" (2 Tim. 3:15).

Painful Parting

While Timothy is often intricately linked to his mother in Scripture, he was called to separate from his mother and spread the gospel message as a missionary. No doubt this was a painful parting. It's not easy for any mother to let her children leave the nest, much less to send them off to foreign lands among people who might be hostile to them and the message they bear. However, based on Eunice's character, I'm sure she was proud of God's call on her son's life and supportive of his ministry. Like a healthy geranium, Eunice was willing to allow the severing of son from mother to promote more growth. Timothy, who accompanied Paul on his missionary journeys, was cut away from his home and his faithful mother and grandmother so that others could be added to the family of faith. The letters written by Paul to Timothy continue to inspire believers throughout the world. Truly, Eunice's willingness to let Timothy go was a sweet sacrifice for the Lord.

How Does Your Garden Grow?

Life has a way of getting too hot to handle. Perhaps the geranium in your garden of friends is experiencing the heat of family heartache—a prodigal child, an unbelieving spouse or ailing parents. Or maybe you're feeling like a geranium bearing the heat with seemingly no relief in sight. Take heart! Here are some helpful hints to help a geranium thrive.

Stay Rooted

One geranium expert says, "Geraniums in containers tend to bloom better when slightly pot-bound."[3] In other words, geraniums grow best when their roots are intertwined. This is also true of our geranium friends. When situations get tangled up, it's easy to detach and stay away from friends who are rooted in the faith. It could be that we feel embarrassed by the situation we're facing. Other times we're simply too tired to make the effort to stay in touch with Christian friends. However, God's Word clearly states that we grow best when we maintain fellowship with other believers. The writer of Hebrews cautioned against "forsaking the assembling of ourselves together, as is the manner of some, but exhorting one another, and so much the more as you see the Day approaching" (Heb. 10:25). Especially when circumstances get snarly, we need to surround ourselves with faithful friends who will encourage us to stay the course and keep our eyes on Christ.

Stop Pests

Noted horticulturists point out that "one of the main problems encountered in production of geraniums is plant diseases. . . . An integrated pest management approach should be used to manage the disease problems associated with geraniums."[4] As believers, we also need an integrated pest-management approach to keep us spiritually strong and healthy. The greatest disease known to humankind is sin. When heated circumstances arise, even the strongest Christians can fall into "pesty" sinful patterns such as self-reliance

The gospel is like a fresh, mild, and cool air in the extreme heat of summer, a solace and comfort in the anguish of the conscience.

MARTIN LUTHER

(thinking we can solve our own problems), self-pity (focusing on self, not others) and self-indulgence (turning to the world's ways for comfort). Fortunately, Jesus provides the antidote to sin: confession. "If we confess our sins, He is faithful and just to forgive us our sins and to cleanse us from all unrighteousness" (1 John 1:9). If life has grown so hot that you've become plagued with personal sin, turn to Christ. He will gladly forgive you and restore you to spiritual health.

Start Praying

The geraniums in my garden of friends have helped me to learn that the only way I'll ever get through a heated situation is on my knees. Kristi, my mom, and the other geraniums in my garden of friends have long practiced praying when life gets tough. In one situation, things were so difficult that my mom didn't know what to pray, so she recited Scripture and sang hymns, finding comfort in God's Word and songs of praise. If life is too much for you to bear and you don't know what to pray, try singing a song or reciting Scripture. You'll be amazed at the peace that invades your heart.

A kindergarten class was touring a fire station as part of their fire safety instruction. The fireman explained what to do in case of a fire. He said, "First, go to the door and feel the door to see if it's hot." Then he said, "Fall to your knees. Does anyone know why you ought to fall to your knees?" One of the kids piped up, "Sure, to start praying to ask God to get you out of this mess!" If the fires of life are closing in, follow this child's advice: Start praying. God may not take away the heat, but He'll make it bearable.

Digging Deeper

1. We've discovered that our geranium friends are often forced to stand alone. Read Hebrews 13:5-6 and then answer the related questions.

   Describe the comfort and companionship to be found in Christ.

   How might this knowledge help you when you're feeling alone?

2. Eunice, a biblical geranium, faced the heat of marriage to an unbeliever. Read 1 Peter 3:1-4 and then explain how a believing wife should witness to her unbelieving husband.

3. Journal about a time when you felt like a geranium. When the heat was on, how did you stay rooted in the faith?

4. One thing that weakens geraniums is pests. If you have allowed self-reliance, self-pity or self-indulgence to swarm your life, write a prayer, confessing your sin to God and asking Him to cleanse you of unrighteousness. Ask Him to help you develop an "integrated pest-control" system.

Daisies

A young girl, looking at the teacher's spectacles perched atop her nose, whispered to her friend, "Wouldn't you hate to wear glasses all the time?" "No-o-o," the friend answered, "not if I had the kind my grandma wears. She sees how to fix things; she sees lots of things to do on rainy days; she sees when people are tired or sad and what will make them feel better; and she always sees what you meant to do even if you didn't do it right. She just looks at things differently from the way other people do. I think it's because of her glasses."[1]

The daisies in my garden of friends are like this wonderful grandmother. They see the world in a positive way. The word "daisy" comes from the Old English "day's eye."[2] This name was bestowed because the daisy opens when the sun comes up and closes at night. In other words, it basks in the sunlight. Our daisy friends are like the flower: cheerful, optimistic and sunny. I like to think that what makes a person a daisy is that she sees things through Son glasses.

You can easily recognize the daisies in your heart's garden by these characteristics. They

- See the bright side
- Show a heart of gold
- Spread cheer

Since my temperament tends to be slightly melancholy, I'm thankful that God has placed several people in my life who are like the daisy. They are the friends who remind me to look at things through God's eyes rather than from my limited human perspective. They bloom all season and are dependable year after year. The daisies are not especially needy, not very flashy and not temperamental. Daisies are the "through thick and thin" friends—the ladies I rely on to keep growing and blooming, making my garden a happy place in which to be.

The Garden in My Heart

The daisies in my life are the eternal optimists who look on the bright side of every circumstance. *Webster's 1913 Dictionary* defines an optimist as "one who holds the opinion that all events are ordered for the best; one who looks on the bright side of things, or takes hopeful views." But daisies in God's garden aren't optimists without cause. They live by the credo of Romans 8:28: "We know that all things work together for good to those who love God, to those who are the called according to His purpose."

Sees the Bright Side

One of my friends, Julie, is an optimist like the daisy. She has developed the ability to view things in the best possible light because she trusts God's perfect plan. It could be because her husband is a university basketball coach and she's a natural cheer-leader. Even if the team is losing, Julie will say, "God's using this to train the team and make them strong. Everything will be OK."

Julie has also been my personal cheerleader. She was on my team when we brought Joni Eareckson Tada to town. She and our friend Marie took on the roles of Aaron and Hur during that season of my life, holding up my arms so that we could accomplish a big task. We had set a date and sold out tickets for Joni's *The God I Love.* Two weeks before the event, I received a phone call from Joni's assistant, Judy. She said, "Joni's broken her leg. Her doctor has told her she can't come as scheduled. We'll need to rethink the conference." Of course, my first and greatest concern was for Joni's well-being. But then, in my melancholy way, I began to think of all the people who would be disappointed, of the enormous amount of work it would take to cancel the event, and of the possible financial repercussions for our organization. My mental list of the downside grew longer and longer. I called Julie and she immediately said, "God has something amazing in store. Let's pray and see what it is."

> *Cheerfulness and contentment are great beautifiers and are famous preservers of good looks.*
>
> CHARLES DICKENS

She was right—God did have something amazing in store. We were able to reschedule Joni's visit. After much prayer and consultation, we secured a larger venue and opened our previously "women's only" event to men as well. Many doubters told us that we could not hope to regain momentum or sell more tickets. But Julie kept her Son glasses on and said, "I know God has a plan. Let's go for it!" And she was right: Not only did Joni come several weeks later, but we also sold twice the number of tickets than we had initially planned. God truly did work things out for our good and His glory.

The German poet Goethe immortalized the daisy when he wrote of Marguerite's desire to know whether Faust really loved her. She plucked the daisy petals and chanted, "He loves me. He loves me not." But daisies like Julie know beyond a shadow of a doubt that God loves them and will work everything out in the best possible way.

Shows a Heart of Gold

Take a moment and picture a daisy in your mind. One of the first things you'll imagine is the golden yellow center from which the petals radiate. In my mind's eye, the daisy's beauty begins with a heart of gold. One person comes immediately to mind when I think of this personal attribute: my friend Barb. Barb wants to please God and knows that pleasing Him involves ministering to others. Barb is tireless when it comes to helping people. At the drop of a hat, she'll happily babysit kids, cook a meal or intercede in prayer. Barb has taught me that a heart of gold springs from a heart for God. The daisy with a heart of gold is like the virtuous woman whose "worth is far above rubies" (Prov. 31:10).

Spreads Cheer

Joy radiates from our daisy friends as white petals radiate from the golden center of the flower. Carmen, another of the friends in my chain of daisies, is probably the most radiant, cheerful woman I know. I can't think of a time when I've seen Carmen despondent or downcast. Perhaps her joy springs from the fact that she was rooted in the ways of the world until she was an adult. But after almost losing everything in her business, she gained everything by becoming a bright flower in God's garden and discovered that "the joy of the LORD is [our] strength" (Neh. 8:10).

Just as daisies spread cheer whether they are growing wild in a meadow or enhancing a floral bouquet, our daisy friends possess a joy that is contagious and that cascades to everyone they encounter.

In God's Garden

One of the most beautiful daisies in God's garden was an early believer named Dorcas, also called Tabitha.

Her Heart Was in the Right Place

If the Early Church had been looking for a Proverbs 31 woman who extends her hand to the poor and "reaches out her hands to the needy" (Prov. 31:20), Tabitha perfectly fit the bill. In her hometown of Joppa, Tabitha was well known for having a heart of gold. Scripture tells us that "this woman was full of good works and charitable deeds which she did" (Acts 9:36). Another way to describe her would be as a woman full of mercy and compassion—she was moved with pity toward those less fortunate than herself. However, not only did she feel pity, but she also took action, giving out of her own resources to help the poor. As a disciple of Christ, Tabitha's heart was in the right place, because she displayed Christ's love to those in need.

Her Death Brought Grief

Clearly, Tabitha spread joy. Though Scripture does not tell us in so many words, we can presume that she radiated cheer to those around her, based on the display of grief at her death. The Bible recounts how, after Tabitha took sick and died, the disciples called for Peter. When he arrived, "all the widows stood by him weeping, showing the tunics and garments which Dorcas had made while she was with them" (Acts 9:39). Her life reveals that those who spread the most joy are mourned the most deeply.

Her Resurrection Spread Hope

The story of Tabitha does not end with death—it looks on the bright side, as all daisies should. Let's read the conclusion of Tabitha's story to learn more:

> Peter put them all out, and knelt down and prayed. And turning to the body he said, "Tabitha, arise." And she opened her eyes, and when she saw Peter she sat up. Then he gave her his hand and lifted her up; and when he had called the saints and widows, he presented her alive. And it became known throughout all Joppa, and many believed on the Lord (Acts 9:40-42).

No biblical truth is more optimistic than the principle of the resurrection from the dead. This magnificent manifestation of God's power over death spread like a blanket of daisies to those around Tabitha.

It is well known that the Sadducees in Christ's time did not believe in the resurrection. My pastor explained, "That's why they were sad, you see." But Tabitha proved that God can and will raise His people from the dead. This is one of the key reasons why all of us ought to be daisies in God's garden: We can always look on the bright side toward a bright future in eternity with our Lord.

How Does Your Garden Grow?

One daisy enthusiast said, "Daisies are an easy to grow perennial that brightens the flower garden and is great for indoor vases and arrangements. . . . Daisies are among the most popular of flowers . . . and they are perfect for beginning gardeners and those whose thumb is not too green!"[3] But just because daisies are easy to grow doesn't mean we can over-look them completely. We need to take the time to cultivate our daisy friends because they add hope, beauty and joy to our lives.

Just as a good real-estate agent will tell you that the secret to good sales is "location, location, location," gardeners know that the secret to any plant's success is "soil, soil, soil." The key to growing beautiful daisies is to sow them in good soil.

Matthew 13 gives us great insight into gardening souls in good soil. Desiring to teach His disciples about the kingdom of heaven, Jesus told the parable of the sower (see vv. 24-32). He explained how a farmer planted seed in four kinds of soil: sideline soil, stony soil, sticky soil and spiritual soil. Of course, only the spiritual soil thrived. We can help our daisy friends flourish by taking soil samples.

> *Everything is okay in the end. If it's not okay, then it's not the end.*
>
> ANONYMOUS

Sideline Soil

Jesus taught that along the wayside, birds (here a symbol of sinfulness or satanic influence) can carry away the seed of God's Word so that it never gets a chance to bloom. If you have become aware that a daisy in your life has fallen into a sinful habit, don't hesitate to go and talk to her, lest her faith take wings and fly away. Paul tells us how to go about this: "If a man [or woman] is overtaken in any trespass, you who are spiritual restore such a one in a spirit of gentleness, considering yourself lest you also be tempted" (Gal. 6:1).

Stony Soil

Jesus also explained about seed on stony soil: "[She] who received the seed on stony places, this is [she] who hears the word and immediately receives it with joy; yet [she] has no root in [her]self, but endures only for a while. For when tribulation or persecution arises because of the word, immediately [she] stumbles" (Matt. 13:20-21). If a daisy in your life has a heart that is turning to stone because she's being persecuted for her faith, remind her of Jesus' words: "Blessed are those who are persecuted for righteousness' sake, for theirs is the kingdom of heaven" (Matt. 5:10). When you help your friend look beyond today's troubles toward tomorrow's promises, you're helping her stay on the right path.

> *My friend is he who will tell me my faults in private.*
>
> SOLOMON IBN GABIROL

Sticky Soil

Jesus further described the characteristics of the person whose seed was planted among the thorns or, as I call it, "sticky" soil: "[She] hears the word, and the cares of this world and the deceitfulness of riches choke the word, and [she] becomes unfruitful" (Matt. 13:22). If your daisy isn't blooming in the way she once did, perhaps she is in sticky soil: She's taking her focus off heavenly treasure in order to gaze upon earthly things. In a loving way, you can remind her of Jesus' command to "lay up for yourselves treasures in heaven, where neither moth nor rust destroys and where thieves do not break in and steal. For where your treasure is, there your heart will be also" (Matt. 6:20). When you remind her of heavenly treasures, the things of Earth will grow strangely dim.

Spiritual Soil

Jesus went on to explain that "[she] who received seed on the good ground is [she] who hears the word and understands it, who indeed bears fruit and produces: some a hundredfold, some sixty, some thirty" (Matt. 13:23). God's Word is like a seed that grows in our lives, allowing us to bear spiritual fruit. Take the time to plant God's Word firmly in your daisies' hearts and minds by encouraging them to attend a church that teaches the Bible and by attending Bible study with them and talking often about what Scripture means to you. Pray for the soil of your daisies' hearts: that the birds won't come to carry the Word away; that their hard times won't produce hard hearts; that the cares of the world won't choke out their joy. Pray that the Word of God will take root in fertile soil and grow abundantly in their lives.

You will never develop eyestrain by looking on the bright side of life.

ANONYMOUS

A Christian legend is told of how the wise men, on their journey to honor the newborn King, asked for a sign that would show them the way to where He was. As they looked down, they spied a carpet of small white daisies near a stable in Bethlehem. They immediately recognized how the flower resembled the star that had led them, and they rejoiced as the door opened to reveal the baby Jesus who had come to save the world.[4]

The daisy in our garden of friends displays a bright outlook, a heart of gold and a cheerful disposition that points to our Savior. Won't you strive to be a daisy growing in the gardens of your friends, brightening their day by displaying Christ's love?

Digging Deeper

1. The daisy has a way of looking at life through "Son glasses." Which of your friends would you call a daisy? How has she exhibited this ability to see things through God's eyes?

2. Faithful daisies apply the Romans 8:28 principle to their lives. Reread this life-changing verse and then answer the following questions:

   Fill in the key word that proves Romans 8:28 is a certainty in the believer's life:

   "We _____that all things work together for good to those who love God, to those who are the called according to His purpose."

   Explain how many things God will work together for our good and how this personally brings you comfort.

   For whom does God work all things together? Can you say with confidence that this includes you?

3. Rewrite Romans 8:28 into a personal proclamation, entrusting a difficult situation to God's good work. For example, "I know that God will work my difficult financial situation out for good because I love Him and am called according to His purpose."

4. The key to growing daisies is good soil.

   Which soil does your heart most resemble right now: sideline, stony or sticky?

   Indicate what steps you'll take so that your soul's soil becomes more spiritual:

   ❐ Sideline—Confess your personal sin and turn away from it.

   ❐ Stony—Pray that God will "take the heart of stone out of your flesh and give you a heart of flesh" (Ezek. 36:26).

   ❐ Sticky (thorny)—Change your mind about earthly things and "desire a better, that is, a heavenly country" (Heb. 11:16).

Pansies

Author John Powell tells of a wise teacher who was speaking to a group of eager young students. He gave them the assignment to go out and find a small, unnoticed flower somewhere. He asked them to study the flower for a long time. "Get a magnifying glass and study the delicate veins in the leaves, and notice the nuances and shades of color. Turn the leaves slowly and observe their symmetry. And remember that this flower might have gone unnoticed and unappreciated if you had not found and admired it." After the class returned, the teacher observed, "People are like that. Each one is different, carefully crafted, uniquely endowed. But you have to spend time with them to know this."[1]

There are some flowers in our garden that we don't spend long periods of time with, but we're so glad for the time we have had with them. These flowers are known as annuals. A gardening expert says, "An annual is a plant that completes its life cycle, from seed to bloom and back to seed again, all in a single growing season."[2] Though bright and beautiful, these flowers generally don't grow back every year, so they need to be replaced.

My favorite annual is the pansy. I love pansies because they restore color to the landscape following the long, dark winter months. Just picture the winter landscape: The earth has gone to sleep under a drab brown blanket; trees stand naked, stripped of their hopeful green leaves; flowers hide their heads underground, waiting for the warm sun to coax them outside to play. Nowhere in this dismal scene is there a hint of color—but wait! You drive by the local nursery and there they are: cheerful pansies smiling at you, begging you to take them home. So you buy a flat (or two) of the colorful end-of-winter wonders and plant them around the borders of your sidewalk or in your lonely ceramic pots. Now when you look out, you're greeted with glorious color blazing against winter's stark background.

We all have friends who are like the pansies. They come into our lives during dark or drab seasons. They are beautiful, bright and interesting, yet they may not return to grow in the garden next year. Maybe they're the moms at the PTA, the women at a Pilates class, coworkers in the office next door or even ladies in your Bible study. You grow close for a time, but then circumstances pull you apart—your kids change schools, you get a new job, the new Bible study starts. Soon you discover there are new pansies to be planted, a new crop of ladies to befriend. These friendships, though sometimes short-lived, are important and should never be overlooked, because they teach us to love others while we have the chance.

The pansies in our garden of friends can be recognized by some common characteristics. They

- Are full of color
- Fill in the gaps
- Fulfill a divine purpose

Paul tells us, "As we have opportunity, let us do good to all, especially to those who are of the household of faith" (Gal. 6:10). Pansies remind us to appreciate and nurture every flower in our garden, even if they're only in our lives for a short while.

The Garden in My Heart

Pansies are exuberant flowers that come in a multitude of colors. Many people think the dark centers in the flowers resemble little faces. The word "pansy" can be traced back to the French word *pensée*, meaning "thought" or "remembrance."[3] What a delight to remember the lovely faces of the charming pansies in my heart's garden.

Full of Color

One of those pansies is my colorful friend Marita Littauer. You always know when Marita enters a room: She dresses in vibrant hues and always has a bright smile on her face. Though I don't see her very often, she's lifted my spirits during some very dark times.

Several years ago, I entered a spiritual winter season in which I grew depressed. When my doctor asked what my depression looked like, I said, "Everything just seems gray and bland." She urged me to take some positive steps to emerge from the darkness. One thing she encouraged me to do was focus on something to help others. I prayerfully began to pursue teaching and writing. I signed up for the CLASS seminar led by Marita and her mom, Florence, a dynamic duo who seek to encourage and educate Christian writers and speakers.

Over the next few months, Marita encouraged me to pursue writing Bible studies for publication. She believed in what I was doing and helped me gain the confidence to pursue the dream.

When I'd see her in church, she would ask, "Have you written your proposal yet?" Her enthusiasm propelled me to take the next step. When the proposal was ready, she took it to various publishers and urged them to consider it. Nine months later, Lenya and I had written and published an award-winning Bible study called *Pathway to God's Treasures: Ephesians.* I'm so grateful that Marita came into my life at just the right time and painted a rainbow of hope back in my heart.

> *The moment may be temporary, but the memory is forever.*
>
> ANONYMOUS

Fill In the Gaps

Just as pansies fill in when dormant perennials are not in bloom, some friends fill in the gaps when something is missing. Early in my winter season, I began to isolate myself from friends and social situations. One of my few activities was attending a study called Bible Study Fellowship. There I met a woman named Debbie. Our kids went to the same school and we hit it off right away. She soon discovered that I was wrestling with God's will and wondering whether I could endure the personal pain I felt. Debbie phoned and quoted precious words of wisdom and encouragement: "The will of God will never take you where His grace will not keep you." This insight, so old to others, was new to me. It was like I'd been drowning and had suddenly been thrown a lifeline. Debbie helped me to grasp the depths of God's grace and His ability to give me peace amid the storms. I still keep in my Bible the scrap of paper on which I scribbled this spiritual principle—just in case life begins to turn gray again.

After a while, our family moved to a different neighborhood and I lost touch with Debbie. But I'll always remember how, during a time of doubt, she stood in the gap and planted God's love and comfort into my soul.

Fulfill a Divine Purpose

For me, pansies serve a key purpose: They hold the promise that spring is coming. During my winter season, my friend Cris fulfilled such a purpose in my life. She encouraged me to focus on the Lord, trusting Him to take care of everything else. She helped me see that I was trying to do too much; I needed to let some things go. While I was high-strung, Cris was laid-back. When I obsessed over a clean house, Cris reminded me to focus on a clean heart. When I stressed out over what others thought of me, Cris put things in perspective: "What's most important is what God thinks of you."

We all need friends who redirect us to a heavenly point of view when we're stuck in the muck of the world. Though Cris has moved on in her life, I value the time we had together and treasure the way she reminded me to keep the divine in mind.

In God's Garden

There are several women who can be deemed pansies in God's garden. They are the women, some only mentioned fleetingly, who enhance our understanding of Jesus Christ through the color and depth of their devotion.

She Sat at His Feet

Mary, the sister of Martha and Lazarus, added color to Jesus' life by comforting Him in one of His darkest times. Jesus had come to Jerusalem knowing He would ultimately be handed over to the authorities and crucified as a criminal. Aware that the chief priests and Pharisees were plotting against Him, Jesus sought refuge in Bethany. At the supper table, we're told that "Mary took a pound of very costly oil of spikenard, anointed the feet of Jesus, and wiped His feet with her hair. And the house was filled with the fragrance of the oil" (John 12:3). When some rebuked Mary for the "waste," Jesus said, "Why do you trouble the woman? For she has done a good work for Me. For you have the poor with you always, but Me you do not have always" (Matt. 26:10-11).

Sitting at the feet of Jesus was a familiar place to find Mary, but her outpouring of love at a dark time ministered to her Lord. Her gesture encourages us to truly appreciate those we love while they are with us. More importantly, her deed compels us to make an effort to sit at Christ's feet and pour out the love in our hearts.

She Gave All She Had

Just as some pansies are in the garden to fill in gaps, the selfless act of a nameless widow gave Jesus the perfect opportunity to fill in His teaching with the important principle of giving whole-heartedly. Jesus was teaching in the Temple when "He looked up and saw the rich putting their gifts into the treasury, and He saw also a certain poor widow putting in two mites" (Luke 21:1-2). Jesus used this woman's overflowing generosity to teach a key lesson: "Truly I say to you that this poor widow put in more than all. . . . She out of her poverty put in all the livelihood that she had" (vv. 2-4). To this day, the story of the widow and her two mites serves as an example to give wholeheartedly.

They Shared the Good News

The pansies in God's garden also fulfilled a divine purpose. Many of the women following Christ were the last to leave the cross. Scripture tells us that at the crucifixion, "Many women who followed Jesus from Galilee, ministering to Him, were there looking on from afar, among whom were Mary Magdalene, Mary the mother of James and Joses, and the mother of Zebedee's sons" (Matt. 27:55-56). But their purpose was not just to witness Christ's death. These women were also first at the tomb: "Now after the Sabbath, as the first day of the week began to dawn, Mary Magdalene and the other Mary came to see the tomb" (Matt. 28:1). These women heard firsthand from the angel of the Lord that Jesus "is not here; for He is risen, as He said" (Matt. 28:6). Then they were given a divine purpose: "Go quickly and tell His disciples that He is risen from the dead" (Matt. 28:7). The divine purpose of every believer can be found in that statement. Our goal as women in God's garden should be to spread the divine hope of new life in Christ.

Man shall commune with all creatures to his profit, but enjoy God alone. That is why no human being can be a permanent source of happiness to another.

DAG HAMMARSKJÖLD

Though many people undervalue pansies, viewing them as short-lived flowers that only have a brief growing season, the truth is that without pansies the winters would seem endless. The women who bloom like pansies in our lives bring color when life is cold and gray; they willingly step in when others walk away, and serve as messengers of hope when things seem hopeless.

How Does Your Garden Grow?

Some of the friends you now consider perennials may, in fact, really be annuals like the pansy. We don't always know how long a friend will stay in our lives, so we should appreciate the

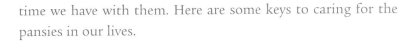

time we have with them. Here are some keys to caring for the pansies in our lives.

Warm by Cooling

Pansy experts say, "Pansies thrive in cool weather. They will bloom any time that the temperature is above freezing. Their peak bloom is in spring. They fade and should be discarded with the start of hot summer weather."[4]

The pansy is the flower in our garden of friends who likes to keep it cool. I've had some friends who just weren't able to stand beside me when situations got too hot. I've discovered that sometimes they just feel the pain of others too deeply and it's safer for them to cool the relationship when circumstances heat up. While it's true that "a friend loves at all times" (Prov. 17:17), it is good for us to understand our friends' capacity for pain. We can be a good friend to the pansies in our lives by graciously releasing them from obligations when things get too hot and by realizing that their detachment doesn't diminish their love for us.

Protect by Covering

Our pansy planters caution, "After the ground is thoroughly frozen, the pansies should receive some protection."[5] While pansies may seem to be a hardy plant, they do need protection. So, too, our colorful friends need us to protect them. "To protect" means to "to cover or shield from exposure, injury, damage, or destruction."[6] Paul encourages believers to arm themselves with "the shield of faith with which you will be able to quench all the fiery darts of the wicked one" (Eph. 6:16). Roman shields were designed to interlock with the shields of fellow soldiers to provide unified protection from flying arrows. If your pansy friend is being assaulted by darts of doubt or discouragement, lock shields with her and cover her with your faith in the God who can defeat any enemy.

Add by Subtracting

Our pansy experts tell us that when pansies "show a tendency to produce runners, and the branches become long, they may be cut back, whereupon the plant will branch out and produce another crop of bloom."[7] In God's economy, sometimes we can only add blossoms by subtracting stems. Jesus said, "Every branch in Me that does not bear fruit He takes away; and every branch that bears fruit He prunes, that it may bear more fruit" (John 15:2). Do you have a friend who is pursuing too many things, growing in too many directions? Perhaps you can encourage her, as my friend Cris encouraged me, to let God prune away some unnecessary pursuits in order to grow stronger in her faith.

It may be bittersweet to think of those friends who were in your life for only a season. But one of the wondrous things I've discovered about pansies is that they may return when least expected. Looking out at my winter garden this week, I was surprised to see voluntary pansy petals popping up their hopeful heads.

The same is true with my pansy friends: I may think they've faded from my life only to have them unexpectedly return. For instance, my friend Debbie, whom I had completely lost touch with, called not long ago. Since then, we've met for coffee and reconnected, easily picking up where we left off.

Out in the garden, wee Elsie
 Was gathering flowers for me;
"Oh, mamma," she cried, "hurry, hurry,
 Here's something I want you to see!"

I went to the window. Before her
  A velvet-winged butterfly flew,
And the pansies themselves were no brighter
  Than this beautiful creature, in hue.

"Oh, isn't it pretty?" cried Elsie,
  With eager and wondering eyes,
As she watched it soar lazily upward
  Against the soft blue of the skies.
"I know what it is, don't you, mamma?"—
  Oh, the wisdom of these little things
When the soul of a poet is in them—
  "It's a pansy—a pansy with wings!"[8]

God is able to restore relationships in His perfect way and in His perfect time. Let this sweet poem remind you that though they may leave for a while, God can always stir the colorful pansy to fly back into your life at just the right time.

Digging Deeper

1. Describe some of the pansies in your heart's garden. Journal about someone who:

   Was full of color:

   Filled in a gap:

   Fulfilled a divine purpose:

2. Solomon wrote, "To everything there is a season, a time for every purpose under heaven. . . . A time to plant, and a time to pluck what is planted" (Eccles. 3:1-2). What does this Scripture teach you about those people who are only in your life for a short time?

3. Read Colossians 3:8-9 and then complete the following exercise:

   List the things believers should put off or prune away.

Explain which of these needs to be pruned from your life.

4. Now read Colossians 3:12-13 and complete the exercise.

List the things believers should put on or plant into their lives.

Which of these do you most need in your life?

5. Journal a prayer, asking God to help you prune away those things that displease Him. Ask Him to plant those spiritual attributes in your heart so that your life can blossom into a blessing.

Forget-Me-Nots

Little Amy was a shy, awkward girl who was ostracized by her classmates. Nevertheless, she wanted to make a valentine for everyone in her class. Her mom's heart sank when she heard Amy's words because she didn't want her little girl to be hurt if Amy's classmates didn't reciprocate; but she decided to go along with her daughter's wishes and purchased paper, glue, lace and crayons. For three weeks, night after night, Amy painstakingly made 35 personalized valentines.

On February 14, the little girl carefully put the valentines in her backpack and cheerfully headed for school. Amy's mom watched her go with a feeling of sadness.

That afternoon, when Amy's mom heard the children returning home, she ran to peek out the window. Sure enough, the kids were walking up the street, ignoring Amy. But when the door opened, Amy's face was aglow. "Not a one—not a one," the little girl repeated over and over, then added, "I didn't forget a one, not a single one!"[1]

I'm blessed with friends whom I see as forget-me-nots in my heart's garden, because they have the amazing ability to remember every single one of their friends. Forget-me-nots are unmistakable bright blue flowers. They grow in abundance in many gardens—often appearing unexpectedly as volunteers to establish colorful clusters among the planted flowers. Some gardeners get frustrated with these small blue gems because forget-me-nots refuse to leave a landscape, even when an effort is made to dig them out.

My forget-me-nots are the friends who, though they've moved away geographically, have not moved away emotionally. Unlike little Amy, who was thoughtlessly forgotten by people she held dear, forget-me-nots in a garden of friends maintain reciprocal relationships: They don't forget their friends, and their friends don't ever forget them.

You can recognize forget-me-nots by a few common characteristics. They

- Bloom where they're planted
- Have been transplanted to a new location
- Are permanently implanted in our hearts

The chorus to Michael W. Smith's song *Friends* captures the beauty of forget-me-nots: "Friends are friends forever if the Lord's the lord of them."[2]

The Garden in My Heart

I've told you about my violet friend Christy, but let me tell you more about her sister, Lori, one of the forget-me-nots in my heart's garden.

Bloom Where They're Planted

In high school, Lori and I were close friends. But in our junior year, Lori experienced a radical conversion to Christianity. She became a "Jesus Freak," and our fun-loving group of friends grew uncomfortable around her.

Lori bloomed in her newfound faith. Though I had backslidden and was a party girl throughout high school and college, Lori never gave up on our friendship. She would give me Christian albums as gifts and invite me to church events, hoping to rekindle my faith. When she moved to California with her husband, she stayed in touch with me through cards and made sure we reconnected on visits home. When I finally rededicated my life to Christ, I thanked her for having tenaciously prayed for me for so many years. To this day, though we're separated by many miles, we hold one another dear in our hearts.

Transplanted to Other Locations

I became friends with another forget-me-not, Vicki, soon after I rededicated my life to Christ. We met while waiting to pick up our children from Sunday School. We were both pregnant, and our burgeoning bellies instigated a conversation that formed the basis for a close friendship. We started spending many hours hanging out at one another's houses; we prayed and talked about what God was doing in our lives. God joined our families together: I love her kids and she loves mine; our husbands get along great; and we share our most intimate secrets. Vicki and her husband, Mike, even asked Kerry and me to be guardians of their children if something happened to them. Needless to say, I was devastated when Mike's job transferred them to El Paso. Vicki said, "I can't believe I have to live in Texas!" I assured her it was fine—after all, I was Texas born and bred. "That's what worries me!" she jokingly replied.

But Vicki was determined to bloom, even if she was transplanted. She and Mike immediately searched out a Bible teaching church and volunteered to work in the children's ministry. Vicki settled in to a new life in a new locale: working, raising her kids and being a loving wife. Then Mike got transferred again.

The family moved to Phoenix and once again began the process of finding a home church and participating in the ministry there. From afar, I watched in amazement as Vicki was able to blossom in the various places God planted her.

Permanently Implanted

Amid all of Vicki's changes in location, the affection we hold for one another remains constant. She has been on my prayer list for years, and she, in turn, keeps praying for me. She knows what's going on in my life and supports me any way she can. When my oldest daughter recently graduated from high school, Mike and Vicki came to celebrate with us as members of our family. Though God has providentially allowed her to be transplanted to a new locale, I still consider Vicki to be one of my best friends. I'll always cherish her friendship.

The forget-me-nots in my life have taught me that gone does not necessarily mean forgotten. I've also learned to embrace time spent with my friends who live nearby, because they just might get transplanted to another location.

In God's Garden

As I searched Scripture to find the perfect example of a forget-me-not, I came to realize that ultimately we should remember *all* of the Bible's characters and the lessons they hold for us, either through their good or bad examples. The Bible tells us, "All Scripture is given by inspiration of God, and is profitable for doctrine, for reproof, for correction, for instruction in righteousness, that the man of God may be complete, thoroughly equipped for every good work" (2 Tim. 3:16-17). Every flower in God's garden is memorable in some way.

But to me, the Person who exhibits the greatest characteristics of a forget-me-not is Jesus Christ—the One who came to Earth and blossomed in human form; the One who was physically transplanted to heaven following His death and resurrection; the One who lives in the hearts of His followers forever and will one day rule and reign over everything. He is memorable in so many ways. Philippians 2:7-11 helps us understand that Jesus is completely unforgettable in His humanity, divinity and sovereignty.

> *We all take different paths in life, but no matter where we go, we take a little of each other everywhere.*
>
> TIM MCGRAW

Unforgettable in Humanity

We first notice that Jesus is unforgettable in humanity. Our passage tells us that Jesus "made Himself of no reputation, taking the form of a bondservant, and coming in the likeness of men. And being found in appearance as a man, He humbled Himself and became obedient to the point of death, even the death of the cross" (Phil. 2:7-8).

Though Jesus is equal with God, He willingly chose to experience the humilities of humanity: living as we live, feeling what we feel and suffering the pangs of death. He left the glories of heaven to experience the agonies of Earth. Why would God leave the privileges of heaven? Jesus' high priestly prayer helps us understand the reason why: "Father, I desire that they also whom You gave Me may be with Me where I am, that they may behold

My glory which You have given Me" (John 17:24). Jesus took on human flesh so that His human friends could one day dwell with Him in heaven. Jesus said, "Greater love has no one than this, than to lay down one's life for his friends" (John 15:13). Jesus sacrificed His earthly life so that we might gain eternal life—truly the most memorable act of friendship in history.

Unforgettable in Divinity

Jesus is also unforgettable in divinity. Our passage in Philippians goes on to say, "Therefore God also has highly exalted Him and given Him the name which is above every name" (Phil. 2:9). Jesus Christ's name reveals that He was no mere man: He was and is God made man, completely divine and completely human. The angel Gabriel told the Virgin Mary, "You will conceive in your womb and bring forth a Son, and shall call His name JESUS" (Luke 1:31). Jesus would be miraculously, mysteriously conceived by the Holy Spirit in the womb of a woman, thus taking on our human nature even as He remained our God, our deity. He was given a name that literally means "Jehovah is salvation." While others bore the name "Jesus" or "Joshua" in Scripture, only One who walked the earth was conceived of God; only One was the God-Man able to save souls.

While Jesus was His personal name, Our Lord was also called by an official title: Christ. "Christ" literally means "anointed one." The Greek translation of the Hebrew word "anointed" is *Messiah*.[3]

When Jesus asked Peter the soul searching question, "Who do you say that I am?" (Matt. 16:15), Peter gave the correct answer: "You are the Christ, the Son of the living God" (v. 16). When Jesus was baptized, God proclaimed for all to hear, "You are My beloved Son; in You I am well pleased" (Luke 3:22). Jesus is memorable for having walked the earth as God's only Son, anointed of God, the one and only Savior, the promised

Messiah. God's purpose in sending His Son is clear: "God so loved the world that He gave His only begotten Son, that whoever believes in Him should not perish but have everlasting life" (John 3:16). Never forget that everlasting life comes only from our divine, everlasting friend, Jesus Christ.

Unforgettable in Sovereignty

Jesus is, indeed, unforgettable in both His humanity and His divinity. In addition, He is unforgettable in sovereignty. Philippians 2:10 tells us "that at the name of Jesus every knee should bow, of those in heaven, and of those on earth, and of those under the earth, and that every tongue should confess that Jesus Christ is Lord, to the glory of God the Father."

Many have strived to rule the world: Alexander the Great, who conquered most of the then known world, died an ignominious death at the age of 33, following a drinking binge; Ghengis Kahn, whose name means "universal ruler," consolidated various tribes into a unified Mongolia and then ruthlessly extended his empire across Asia to the Adriatic Sea. He, too, died, unable to conquer death. More recently there was Adolf Hitler. He ruled as dictator of Germany and led the militaristic Nazi party in an attempt to conquer Europe, exterminate the Jews and establish a new world order. Yet Hitler's ambitions were ultimately thwarted, and he committed suicide in a Berlin bunker.

Only One will reign supreme over all nations for eternity. And unlike ruthless world dictators who have sought power using brutal means to accomplish selfish purposes, the prophet Isaiah states that Jesus, the King of kings and Lord of lords "will

> *Good friends are hard to find, harder to leave, and impossible to forget.*
>
> ANONYMOUS

reign in righteousness" (Isa. 32:1).

There is a legend that recounts the return of Jesus to glory after His time on Earth. According to this story, when Jesus arrived in heaven, He still bore the marks of His earthly pilgrimage, with its cruel cross and shameful death. The angel Gabriel approached Him and said, "Master, You must have suffered terribly for men down there." He replied that He had. Gabriel continued, "And do they know and appreciate how much You loved them and what You did for them?" Jesus replied, "Oh, no! Not yet. Right now only a handful of people know." Gabriel was perplexed. He asked, "Then what have You done to let everyone know about Your love for them?" Jesus said, "I've asked my disciples to tell others about Me. Those who are told will tell others, in turn, about Me. And My story will be spread to the farthest reaches of the globe. Ultimately, all of humankind will hear about My life and what I have done."

Gabriel looked rather skeptical and, knowing what poor stuff humans are made of, asked, "But what if the people forget? Haven't You made any other plans?" And Jesus answered, "I haven't made any other plans. I'm counting on them."[4]

Jesus, our human, divine, sovereign Lord is counting on us to remember Him and tell others about Him, the God-Man who will rule and reign in eternity.

How Does Your Garden Grow?

Forget-me-nots are fairly easy to grow, but we can help our forget-me-not friends develop the attributes of Jesus by following a couple of simple steps.

Rejoice in Their Steadfastness

While many people in the world are fickle and display an "out of sight, out of mind" mentality, the forget-me-nots in our garden of friends are steadfast and loyal. One gardener despairingly wrote to her friend about the forget-me-nots in her garden, "They're everywhere! I just can't get rid of them."[5] But I don't believe this is a bad thing—it can be viewed as a positive trait. I've often heard that a true friend is someone who comes in when the rest of the world is going out. You could say that a true friend tenaciously holds on when the rest of the world lets go. Though it may feel stifling when a forget-me-not doesn't give you enough space (flower experts say they don't mind crowding), you can rejoice that your friend is steadfast and unwilling to give up on a precious friendship.

Paul encourages us to "be steadfast, immovable, always abounding in the work of the Lord" (1 Cor. 15:58). Rejoice in the steadfastness of your forget-me-nots; then purpose in your heart to be steadfast in your love for them, knowing that unwavering love makes us more like Christ: "He is the living God, *and steadfast forever*; His kingdom is the one which shall not be destroyed, and His dominion shall endure to the end" (Dan. 6:26, emphasis added).

Respect the Need for Separation

"Perennial Forget-Me-Nots can be propagated by separating clumps of established plants."[6]

Forget-me-nots grow best when their roots are divided and dispersed to grow elsewhere. I've found this to be true in my experience. In retrospect, I can see how I've sometimes grown too dependent on my forget-me-not friends when they are nearby. Often, because I enjoy them so much, I've given them time and energy that should have been given to God instead. I've learned that God sometimes separates me from my friends so that I'll appreciate Him more. Likewise, I've noticed that when my forget-me-nots move out of their comfort zones, they lean more intently on God. Though it is so difficult to face a separation from the forget-me-nots in our garden, we can trust God to meet all of our needs spiritually, emotionally and physically: "God shall supply all your need according to His riches in glory by Christ Jesus" (Phil. 4:19).

Although your heart's garden contains forget-me-nots who can no longer be with you physically, remember that Jesus is the forget-me-not who will never leave nor forsake you. Though now He is absent in body, He is absolutely present in Spirit. As He told His disciples before ascending to heaven, "Lo, I am with you always, even to the end of the age" (Matt. 28:20).

When to the flowers so beautiful,
 The Father gave a name,
Back came a little blue-eyed one,
 All timidly it came.
And standing at its Father's feet,
 And gazing in his face,
It said in low and trembling tones,
 And with a modest grace,
"Dear God, the name thou gavest me,
 Alas, I have forgot."
The Father kindly looked Him down,
 And said, "Forget-me-not."[7]

The world is so empty if one thinks only of mountains, rivers, and cities; but to know someone here and there who thinks and feels with us and though distant, is close to us in spirit— this makes the earth for us an inhabited garden.

JOHANN VON GOETHE

With believing forget-me-nots in our garden of friends, we can look forward to spending eternity together in heaven. This should inspire us to share Christ's love with *all* our friends, so that we never really have to say good-bye only, but rather "See you later." Remember to tell every one of your forget-me-not friends about the Father. As the poet reminds us, though *we* may be forgetful, God in His kindness will never forget about you!

Digging Deeper

1. Who in your garden of friends is the forget-me-not? Journal about how she has been able to bloom wherever God has planted her.

2. We saw that Jesus is the greatest of forget-me-nots. With this in mind, complete the following exercise.

   Fill in the following chart to discover some of the things we should always remember:

Scripture	Benefits of God's Word
Psalm 20:7	
Psalm 105:5	
Acts 20:35	
2 Timothy 2:8	
Revelation 2:5	

   Did one of the above Scriptures cause you to realize that you have forgotten something crucial in your spiritual walk?

How has this reminder encouraged you in your faith?

3. Jesus Christ's names point to His humanity and divinity.

Read Isaiah 9:6 and list some of His other names.

Talk about which of these names you need Jesus to be for you and why.

CHAPTER 10

Desert Flowers

The story is told of two friends who went on a journey through the desert. After walking for days, the friends had such an intense argument that one slapped the other's face. The girl who got slapped was sad; but rather than retaliate, she silently wrote in the sand: *Today my best friend slapped me in the face.* Since they were alone in the desert, the friends were forced to keep walking together. At last they found an oasis. The one who had been slapped ran into the water, forgetting that she didn't know how to swim. As she began to go under, her friend came to her rescue. After recovering from near drowning, the rescued friend wrote on a stone: *Today my best friend saved my life.*

The friend who had slapped and then saved her friend asked, "When I hurt you, you wrote in the sand. But when I helped you, you wrote on a stone. Why?" The other friend replied "When someone harms us, we should write it in sand where the winds of forgiveness can blow through to erase the pain. But when someone assists us, we must engrave it in stone where no wind can ever erase it."[1]

Maybe you have some desert flower friendships that have both hurt and helped you. Our desert friends share common characteristics. They

- Grew up in a stark setting
- Guard feelings
- Are given to a sharp tongue
- Grow deep roots in the faith

How do you care for your desert flower friends? They are often prickly as a cactus, thirsty for love, yet willing to dive in and offer assistance when you need it. The way you treat them is critical not only to their spiritual and emotional development but to your growth as well.

It's important to understand that desert flowers have learned to thrive under hot and dry conditions. Many have deep roots that store water so they can survive drought. Others do not bloom until saturated with rain. A large number of desert plants protect themselves with sharp spines or thorns.[2]

Sometimes life on Earth can seem like a wilderness in which we must learn to thrive under sometimes harsh conditions. While walking in the world's wilderness, I've discovered some beautiful desert plants growing in my garden of friends.

Grew Up in a Tough Setting

One of my desert plant friends is a prickly pear cactus. Prickly pears are covered with spikes, but when they bloom their flowers are big and brilliant. Today in Israel, people born in the land are called *sabras*, or prickly pears, because they are tough on the outside and sweet on the inside. That's like my friend Pia, who grew up in the tough streets of New York. She learned to stick up for herself because she lived in a single-parent household and her mother was at work all day, leaving Pia as the family protector. She can come across as prickly because she speaks her mind regardless of the consequences. The first time we met, she slapped down one of my ideas for a women's retreat. Later, however, she called to give me a Scripture as encouragement. I've learned that when I bring my troubles to Pia, she will blossom into a prayer warrior.

Guard Feelings

Another of the flowers in the desert is the resurrection flower. These flowers are mosslike and bear tiny white flowers that roll up when dry and expand when moist. When rain or dew saturates these flowers, they're resurrected, reemerging to abundant life. I see my friend Linda as a resurrection flower. Linda's childhood was marked by extreme desert conditions. She experienced the death of a parent and was sexually abused by trusted adults. She once told me that she literally felt dead inside until she met Jesus. She had rolled herself around her pain and her past.

> *There is no wilderness like a life without friends.*
>
> BALTASAR GRACIÁN Y MORALES

When the Lord began to shower her with His love and wash her with His Word, she was resurrected to a new life in Christ. Now she pours out God's love to others, allowing God to turn her desert of pain into a paradise of praise.

Given to a Sharp Tongue

The desert willow is another of my favorite desert plants because it blooms despite the heat and looks delicate but is, instead, sturdy. The willow branches bear orchidlike flowers with white edges and magenta throats. Several years ago, I grew close to a woman named Suzette who was like a desert willow. She grew up in the scorching desert of life. During childhood, she didn't receive the water of love and was treated with brutality; nonetheless, she was beautiful, insightful and generous. These qualities drew me into a friendship with her.

Over time, however, bitter roots grew in the soil of our relationship. We sinned against one another by gossiping and trying to influence others to take our sides. I can't speak for her, but I let the roots of bitterness seep deep into my heart. Our friendship became so tangled up and bitter that it died. Sadly, the hurts in our relationship were written in stone.

Grow Deep Roots of Faith

Though my desert flower friends have all come from different backgrounds, they have one thing in common: strong faith in the Lord in spite of, or perhaps because of, the difficult circumstances of their lives. They have rightfully placed their faith not in people but in the living God. Scripture teaches, "Faith is the substance of things hoped for, the evidence of things not seen" (Heb. 11:1). Life on Earth may have been difficult, but my desert flower friends know there is a better world to come, so they can live now in the joy of the Lord.

In God's Garden

Deborah's Devotion

The Bible tells of some beautiful desert plants in God's garden. I think of Deborah as a prickly pear cactus. In Israel during the time of the judges, "Everyone did what was right in his own eyes" (Judg. 17:6). Though she was female, Deborah was given the responsibility of judging God's wayward people. Scripture tells us that "she would sit under the palm tree of Deborah between Ramah and

Bethel in the mountains of Ephraim. And the children of Israel came up to her for judgment" (Judg. 4:5). To understand her personality, you need to understand her name. "Deborah" literally means "wasp"[3]; her story reveals that she was willing to sting if need be, even leading an army to war when the Lord directed. She was uncompromising in her zeal for the Lord, singing, "Let all Your enemies perish, O LORD! But let those who love Him be like the sun when it comes out in full strength" (Judg. 5:31). This godly woman could be prickly, but she also blessed those who followed the Lord.

> *The lives that are getting stronger are lives in the desert, deep-rooted in God.*
>
> OSWALD CHAMBERS

Mary's Miracle

You could view Mary Magdalene as a resurrection plant. Scripture reveals that Jesus "had cast seven demons" from her (Mark 9:9). Imagine Mary's life before her deliverance. She had been a tormented soul who had most likely been ostracized by society. The demons probably had abused her both physically and mentally. She was resurrected, given a new life, through the healing touch of Christ's hand. She bloomed into a pure white flower as she followed Jesus throughout His life. As we've seen, she witnessed His harrowing crucifixion and went to the empty tomb, only to be greeted by angels (see John 20:11-13). The lady whose cruel life had been resurrected by the power of Christ's love was privileged to see the risen Lord and deliver the news of His miraculous reappearance to the disciples (see v. 18).

Conflict Resolution

Two women in the Bible were like desert willows experiencing a desert friendship: Euodia and Syntyche. These women were first-century followers of Christ who attended the church at Philippi. There's every indication that they were dedicated believ-ers. We don't know exactly what caused their relationship to be sticky, but they obviously had a falling-out that not only affected them but also the members of their church. The friendship was so strained that news of the conflict reached Paul's ears in Rome. He wrote to the church and mentioned the women by name in an effort to promote reconcilia-tion: "I implore Euodia and I implore Syntyche to be of the same mind in the Lord" (Phil. 4:2).

> *Friendship is . . . a plant and not a roadside thistle. We must not expect our friend to be above humanity.*
>
> OUIDA

We don't know what issue divided the two women, but we do know that Paul urged them to put their differences aside and become like-minded based on their love for the Lord. The word "like-minded" literally means "to have the same soul and to think the same thoughts."[4] In essence, Paul urged them to become soul sisters.

United in Love

It must have been humiliating to read their names written about in such a negative way in the letter from Paul, but I like to think they took his words to heart. We don't know if these women fol-lowed Paul's advice, but it's nice to think that as followers of Christ, they again became friends.

It's encouraging to know that even women in the Bible had dis-agreements. As Christian women, sometimes our friendships can grow strained, too. We cut one another with our words or roll up our emotions to push others away. We have strong opinions and ideas about how things should work. However, if we remember that we are united in a love for the Lord and we work at remaining soul sisters, our deserts can blossom into loving gardens.

How Does Your Garden Grow?

I'm sure you have desert friends and may even have some desert friendships that have withered away. Here are a few tips to help the desert plants in your garden of friends flourish.

Pray for Them

Perhaps you know someone who is as prickly as a cactus. The care of prickly pears is quite simple: Put them in the sun and don't overwater them. You can care for your prickly friends the same way: Make sure you place them in the Son by praying for them often. And don't saturate them with words or too much attention. As Pia says, if you don't get to the point quickly, it "gets on my last nerve." That's when you might get stung.

Place Boundaries

I imagine that, like me, your garden of friends has a resurrection plant—a person whose life has been so desolate that she's rolled up her emotions. When watered, the resurrection plant puts roots down quickly and spreads over a large space. It may be that a particular friend has come into your life because you've poured out the water of Christian friendship. The best way to care for the resurrection plant is to provide boundaries lest you get overwhelmed by her. In my case, I wasn't very good at setting boundaries with Linda. At one point, I felt inundated with her problems. I needed to pull back from the intensity of the relationship for a time. Today, we still pray for one another and bear one another's burdens, but we have better boundaries.

Don't Prune

Desert willows don't like to be pruned. Unfortunately, I cared for my desert willow, Suzette, in the wrong way. In retrospect, I can see that I pruned her by offering critique when she really needed confirmation. My unwise treatment helped lead to our friendship's demise.

Steps to Healing

As we've seen, desert friendships aren't always the easiest friendships to cultivate. Maybe you've saturated with too much attention someone who doesn't need it. Maybe you've grown cold when your friend needs warm emotion to blossom. It could be that bitterness and unforgiveness have grown between you and a friend, as happened with Suzette and me. Perhaps you've written in sand some things that should have been in stone, and written in stone some things that should have been blown away by the winds of forgiveness.

Fortunately, Jesus gave the disciples insight into how to reconcile a broken relationship: "If you are standing before the altar in the Temple, offering a sacrifice to God, and you suddenly remember that someone has something against you, leave your sacrifice there beside the altar. Go and be reconciled to that person. Then come and offer your sacrifice to God" (Matthew 5:23-25, *NLT*). Let's dissect Christ's words to discover four steps to healing.

Step One: Remember

"Remember that someone has something against you." Often we don't realize until it's too late that bitterness is taking root in our hearts or the heart of another. Scripturally, it is our responsibility to recognize the problem. Here are a few telltale signs that your friendship is in jeopardy:

- *Avoidance.* When you notice a dear friend avoiding your company, it's time to examine the relationship.
- *Attachment to others.* It's healthy to build new friend-ships; but if a close friend is clinging to others while avoiding your company, it's a good indication that something is wrong between you.
- *Anger.* Generally, friends don't respond to one another in anger. If anger bubbles over at unexpected times over insignificant issues, there may be a problem in your friendship—and it's very likely that it's not about what caused the outburst. The first step to solving a problem is recognizing that there is a problem. Recognition should lead to repentance.

Step Two: Repent

"Leave your sacrifice there beside the altar. Go . . . " Repentance implies a change of mind about our behavior; it means that you make a decision to turn and go in the opposite direction. Once you recognize something is wrong, the next course of action is to make it right! To repent spiritually is to acknowledge your sin to God, turn from that sin and ask God's forgiveness. To repent relationally, you must be willing to admit how you've sinned against your friend, purpose not to hurt her again and go to seek her forgiveness. You may not have meant to inflict pain, but if someone you care for has been wounded by your words or deeds, you should try to see the situation through her eyes and ask for-giveness.

On the other hand, if you have been sinned against, lovingly go and confront your friend so that she can repent and not hurt others. Sometimes, the feelings run so deep on both sides that healing comes slowly, if ever. But generally, repentance leads to reconciliation.

Step Three: Reconcile

"Be reconciled to that person." Reconciliation implies a restoration to friendship after enmity. Since God paid the price to reconcile us, His sinful enemies, to Himself through Christ, should we not be willing to take the initiative and reconcile with others?

> *The best way to destroy an enemy is to make him a friend.*
>
> ABRAHAM LINCOLN

Reconciliation is based on forgiveness. If the perfect God can forgive our imperfections, shouldn't we, imperfect as we are, forgive others their shortcomings? Forgiveness means to dismiss an offense. It is a conscious effort on our part to forgive and forget—to allow the relationship to move past the pain toward a better, stronger relationship. In a true friendship, forgiving and being forgiven are great cause for rejoicing.

Step Four: Rejoice

"Then come and offer your sacrifice to God." Our relationships with others directly affect our relationship with God. God asks us to sacrifice our pride to set things right on a relational level before we come to Him on a spiritual level. Then we can rejoice! We can offer beautiful sacrifices to God. The psalmist wrote, "The sacrifice [God wants] is a broken spirit. A broken and repentant heart, O God, you will not despise" (Ps. 51:17, *NLT*). Offering the sacrifice of repentance to God and others is cause for celebration.

In a cemetery in Hanover, Germany, lies a grave where huge slabs of granite and marble were cemented and fastened with heavy steel clasps. It belonged to a woman who did not believe in the resurrection of the dead. Inscribed on the tomb are these words: "This burial place must never be opened." However, over time, a seed began to grow by the gravestones. Eventually, a tree grew and its trunk enlarged, shifting the great slabs so that the steel clasps were wrenched from their sockets. A tiny seed had grown strong enough to push aside the stones.

Though our desert friends may sometimes seem closed off, with time and the seed of God's Word, the relationships can thrive. I believe that even dead relationships can be resurrected. Desert friendships are worth the time and energy—even after a falling-out—to recognize any problem, repent of our part in it and reconcile the relationship. Then we will be free to rejoice when God allows friendships to bloom in a wilderness.[5]

Digging Deeper

1. Ask God to reveal to you who the desert flowers are in your life. Explain what makes your friends like the desert flowers.

   Prickly Pear:

   Resurrection Flower:

2. Now tell about a friendship that has died or is near death, like my story of my desert willow friendship.

3. Paul urged Euodia and Syntyche to "be of the same mind" (Phil. 4:2). Read Romans 12:16-17; then list the dos and don'ts of becoming like-minded.

   Don't
   Do
   Don't
   Do
   Don't
   Do

4. Journal about how you have done some of the don'ts and failed in some of the dos regarding the friendship that is failing.

5. Rewrite Isaiah 51:3 into a personal prayer, asking God to help you heal the friendship and cause it to blossom:

> *He will comfort all her waste places;*
> *He will make her wilderness like Eden, and her desert*
> *like the garden of the LORD;*
> *Joy and gladness will be found in it, thanksgiving and*
> *the voice of melody* (Isa. 51:3).

CHAPTER 11
Wildflowers

Evangelist Dwight Moody's father died when Dwight was only four years old. A month after his father's death, Mrs. Moody gave birth to twins, leaving her with nine mouths to feed and no income. Merciless creditors dogged the widow, repossessing everything they could get their hands on. As if Mrs. Moody didn't have enough trouble, her eldest boy ran away from home. Certain that her son would return, Mrs. Moody placed a light for him in the window each night. Inspired by her faith and prayers, Dwight wrote, "I can remember how eagerly she used to look for tidings of that boy; how she used to send us to the post office to see if there was a letter from him—some night when the wind was very high, and the house would tremble at every gust, the voice of my mother was raised in prayer for that wanderer."

Mrs. Moody's prayers were answered when her prodigal son returned. Dwight remembered, "While my mother was sitting at the door, a stranger was seen coming toward the house; and when he came to the door, he stopped. My mother didn't know her boy. He stood there with folded arms and a great beard flowing down his breast, his tears trickling down his face. When my mother saw those tears, she cried, 'Oh, it's my lost son!' and entreated him to come in. But he stood still! 'No, mother,' he answered, 'I will not come in until I hear that you have forgiven me.'"

Mrs. Moody was only too willing to forgive. She rushed to the door and threw her arms around him. There, in his mother's embrace, the prodigal found forgiveness.[1]

As a former prodigal, there is a special place in my heart for those who have wandered from the faith or have never been planted in God's garden. I look upon these people as wildflowers: They are the friends who don't know the Lord, who grow in the ways of the world.

Wildflowers come in every size, shape and color. They grow from coast to coast and around the world. While there are many varieties of wildflowers, you can recognize the wildflowers in your heart's garden by a few common characteristics. They

- Hunger after unnatural needs
- Harbor some damaging weeds
- Hanker for spiritual seed

Many of the wildflowers in my garden of friends were sown when I was walking on the wild side. It's just like God to use the pain of my past so that others might gain a bright future. I trust that God allowed me to stray so that I can shine God's light upon the wildflowers in my heart. I water the wildflowers with my tears, asking God to draw them to Himself and transplant them home, into His beautiful, well-tended garden.

The Garden in My Heart

While there are many wildflowers in my garden of friends for whom I pray and love, I'd like to give you hope for the wildflowers in your garden by telling you about three flowers God allowed me to help transplant into His garden.

Hunger After Unnatural Needs

One Sunday at church, I was astonished to see a friend from school named Katie sitting in the front row. I knew that Katie had gotten caught up in drugs, feeding her need for a natural—actually, unnatural—high. I consider her a poppy since she developed an addictive cocaine habit that ate away at her soul. Her hair was lank and her eyes dark and sunken in. She looked like a walking corpse. It was hard to focus on the message because I kept my eyes on Katie and prayed, *Oh, Lord, let Your Word sink in.* When the service ended, I hurried to the front of the church to reconnect with my long-lost friend. Katie was sitting in her chair, crying. I hugged her and said, "I'm so glad to see you. How can I help?" She replied, "I want what that pastor was talking about. I need a new life."

Though I'm not an evangelist, I knew God had put me in the right place at the right time. I took a deep breath and said, "Do you want to ask Jesus into your heart? Can I pray with you?" She nodded and we prayed a prayer, planting her as a flower in God's garden.

A few weeks later, I again saw Katie at church. Her hair was full and beautiful. Her skin looked healthy and her eyes were glowing. Though she had walked in some really dark places in her past, she had seen the light and become involved in our community of faith. Her natural cravings had been replaced with a supernatural hunger for God.

Harbor Damaging Weeds

Another wildflower friend of mine, Candace, was going through some difficult times. Like me, she had grown up believing in the Lord but had backslidden during high school. I see her as the wild foxglove that grows along the East and West coasts. A foxglove is the source of digitalis, a drug prescribed to regulate the heart. Sadly, Candace had allowed her heart to be turned away from heavenly treasures and was wholeheartedly seeking material possessions. Unfortunately, her personal drive had driven her husband into the arms of another woman. The weeds of the cares of the world had begun to choke out her hope.

A friend is someone who understands your past, believes in your future, and accepts you today just the way you are.

ANONYMOUS

One day, I invited her to lunch and she started talking about her business success: "I expect to retire before I'm 40. I'm investing so that I'll always have everything I need." I looked at her and said, "You really have everything? You've lost your husband, you're in a battle for your children, and ultimately everything you've gained will burn." Stunned, she sat silent for a few moments. Then tears welled in her eyes and she said, "You're right." Then and there we prayed a prayer of rededication to the Lord. God had turned the heart of another of His prodigals toward home. Today, Candace is involved in her church as a spokeswoman for abstinence education. Though still successful in business, she understands the biblical principle taught by Jesus: "What profit is it to a man if he gains the whole world, and loses his own soul?" (Matt. 16:26).

Hanker for Supernatural Seed

I haven't led a lot of people to the Lord, but He has brought several wildflowers into my life "for such a time as this" (Esther 4:14). My friend Juliana was a wildflower like the sweet alyssum. Alyssum is known for growing in rocky, disturbed ground. I went to a housewarming party at Juliana's new home and soon learned that her marriage was rocky. While showing me her house, she showed me the room where she caught her husband cheating on her. Our conversation revealed that, along with losing her husband, she had lost her way spiritually. She had tried New Age teaching and self-help books, but she told me, "Something's missing—I just don't know what it is." I recognized the gaping spiritual hole in her heart and knew that only God could fill it. I began to talk with her about Jesus' sacrificial love, His faithfulness and His ability to provide for all of her needs. Right away, she said, "I need that." I was privileged to pray with her and introduce her into the kingdom of God.

> *To my God, a heart of flame; to my fellowmen, a heart of love; to myself, a heart of steel.*
>
> SAINT AUGUSTINE OF HIPPO

God soon became the rock-solid foundation of her life. Today she is still like the sweet alyssum, spreading pure white hope to those she meets, showing them how faith can bloom regardless of their difficult circumstances.

I'm not telling you these stories because I'm such a great spokeswoman for the Lord—far from it. There are times when I'm timid and fear that my wildflower friends will reject me because of my faith. There are times when I feel like an utter failure as a witness to my friends. But God is faithful even when we are faithless. He could have chosen to send angels to proclaim

His message—Jesus said even the rocks could cry out about the Savior (see Luke 19:40). But for some reason, God chooses to use weak, human vessels as witnesses of His love and mercy. I believe He wants to use *you* to minister to the wildflowers in your garden of friends. I know that He will provide the opportunities if you'll be faithful to seize the moment and share His love.

In God's Garden

Perhaps the woman who best depicts a wildflower in God's garden is the woman at the well. Her encounter with Jesus reveals that He is "not willing that any should perish but that all should come to repentance" (2 Pet. 3:9). We see in this episode that Jesus welcomes all, knows all and expects us to tell all about Him.

Scripture tells us that following His baptism by John, Jesus "needed to go through Samaria" (John 4:4). In Jesus' day, the people of Samaria were shunned by orthodox Jews because the Samaritans had intermarried with foreigners. Though Samaria was a convenient travel route between Judea and Galilee, the Jews had no dealings with the Samaritans and went out of their way to avoid the territory. Nevertheless, Jesus felt compelled to go there and complete a divine appointment.

Welcomes All

As the story begins, we're told that "a woman of Samaria came to draw water [at Jacob's Well]. Jesus said to her, 'Give Me a drink'" (John 4:7). Jesus' actions were completely unorthodox. In the first place, He had purposely gone to the despised land of the Samaritans. In the second place, He had spoken to a woman—and women, we know, were considered not much more than chattel in those days. Yet Jesus welcomed the company of a desperate woman from a despised race.

Just as wildflowers grow in distant pastures and beside well-traveled highways, Jesus encourages us to "go out into the highways and hedges, and compel them to come in, that my house may be filled" (Luke 14:23). Christ's encounter with the woman at the well proves that no one is out of God's reach no matter where they live or what they've done. God is willing to welcome everyone—regardless of sex, race, creed or color—into His kingdom.

Knows All

We also see that Jesus knows all. He offered to give the thirsty woman living water that would "become [in her] a fountain of water springing up into everlasting life" (John 4:14). But before she could accept this gift, she needed to discover who Jesus was. In order to prove that He was God, Jesus exposed her past. With omniscient knowledge He revealed that she was living with a man to whom she was not married and that she had been married five times before. In perhaps the biggest understatement in Scripture, the stunned woman said, "Sir, I perceive that You are a prophet" (v. 19). Jesus went on to reveal that He was the promised Messiah. The woman "then left her waterpot, went her way into the city, and said to the men, 'Come, see a Man who told me all things that I ever did. Could this be the Christ?'" (vv. 28-29). Jesus knew everything this woman had ever done and He loved her anyway. The same is true for all wildflowers: He knows their past and is willing to cleanse their sin, offering them new life in Him.

Tells All

One thing He asks, once we are transplanted into God's garden, is that we tell others about Him. The woman at the well did just that. Scripture tells us, "Many of the Samaritans of that city

believed in Him because of the word of the woman who testi-
fied" (John 4:39).

What makes a wildflower wild is that it grows on its own,
with no one to tend to it. We can all be viewed as wildflowers
until Jesus comes into our lives and tends to our heart. But once
He takes over as our Master Gardener, we become a beautiful
flower blooming in His garden, now and forever.

How Does Your Garden Grow?

When I had backslidden and was walking in the ways of the world,
the believers in my life ministered to me in three helpful ways.
Here are some keys to cultivating the wildflowers in your life.

Unconditional Love

It has been said that as believers we are to love the sinner and
hate the sin. My parents and grandparents never wavered in their
love for me, despite the sinful lifestyle I had chosen. Just as the
prodigal son was greeted with an embrace by his father, I knew
that I would be met with open arms by my parents and that I was
always welcome at home. The loving-kindness shown to me by
my faithful family members spoke volumes. I believe the
Scripture is true: "God's kindness leads you toward repentance"
(Rom. 2:4, *NIV*). When we love the wildflowers in our life unre-
servedly, we are displaying one of the most amazing facets of
God's love.

Uncompromising Faith

While it is true that we must love unconditionally, we must never
compromise our faith. When I was leading a profligate lifestyle, my
parents refused to condone or support it. When I came home for
visits from college, I knew that I couldn't stay out all night, come

home drunk or bring illegal substances into the house. My family stood up for righteousness, even though I was acting unrighteously. So, too, we should never condone the sinful behavior of those we love. We can be uncompromising in our faith while exhibiting unconditional love. Paul encouraged the Ephesians who were surrounded by idolatry on every side to witness for God with their lifestyles: "See then that you walk circumspectly, not as fools but as wise, redeeming the time, because the days are evil" (Eph. 5:15-16).

Unconventional Witness

Many times people who are not walking with God tune out the Christian lingo we throw at them. They shut their ears to words like "repentance," "substitutionary sacrifice" and "atonement." They roll their eyes if we refer to our "brothers and sisters" in Christ or our "church home." Many times they'll refuse to even enter a church building. Therefore, it's necessary to be unconventional in our approach. Paul said, "I have become all things to all men, that I might by all means save some" (1 Cor. 9:22). I'm not saying that you need to become a drunk in order to win your alcoholic family member to Christ. I am saying that preaching at a prodigal without developing a personal relationship is not very effective. You may need to step out of your comfort zone to reach someone who is living in a danger zone. A philosophy called "one plus one" evangelism has proven to be very powerful: You pour yourself into another's life and trust God to use you to pour out His truth. Jesus left heaven "to seek and to save that which was lost" (Luke 19:10). Should we, His followers, do any less?

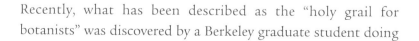

Recently, what has been described as the "holy grail for botanists" was discovered by a Berkeley graduate student doing field work in a California state park. Doctoral candidate Michael Park found a wildflower known as the Mount Diablo buckwheat, thought to be extinct since 1936. The delicate pink flower resembles a small pink powder puff version of baby's breath used in floral arrangements.[2] Now, protected by experts, this delicate endangered wildflower has a chance of survival.

What would a world without wildflowers be like? Perhaps it would be paradise, because the flowers would no longer grow alone in the wild but would be carefully cultivated by the Master Gardener. Think about it, the original Garden of Eden had no wildlife. Every plant, animal and person was purposely placed there by God.

Won't you purpose in your heart to place the seed of the gospel message into the lives of the wildflowers in your heart's garden? They desperately need the Master's care. Perhaps they've only been waiting for *you* to share the good news with them so that they can come under the protection of their heavenly Father and share the joy of eternal life in heaven.

> *Never cease loving a person and never give up hope for him, for even the Prodigal Son who had fallen most low could still be saved.*
>
> SØREN KIERKEGAARD

Digging Deeper

1. Name and describe the wildflowers in your garden of friends.

2. Talk about the time you were a wildflower—before you were saved. How did God reach out to you? Who did He use to minister to your heart?

3. What is keeping you from telling the wildflowers in your garden about Jesus?

   ❏ I'm afraid they'll reject me.
   ❏ They seem happy as they are.
   ❏ I don't see them as much because I hang out with believers now.
   ❏ Other _____

4. According to Matthew 28:19, what action did Jesus command us to take to reach the outside world?

5. When will you "go, therefore" and reconnect with the wildflowers in your garden of friends?

6. Journal a prayer, asking God to give you His words and His wisdom in reaching out to the wildflowers growing in your heart's garden. Ask Him to provide a perfect opportunity for sharing His love.

Sunflowers

For centuries, humans viewed the earth as the center of the universe. They believed that the planet they inhabited was stationary and that the sun and all other heavenly bodies moved around it. But in the sixteenth century, an astronomer named Copernicus observed how the world really turned, and he turned the scientific community upside down with a new theory. He hypothesized that the sun was the fixed point around which the planets revolved, not vice versa. His observations led him to the conclusion that the universe was not geocentric (earth centered), but heliocentric (sun centered). His insights changed our understanding of the physical reality of the universe. However, his ideas were rejected by many. Galileo, who embraced the Copernican theory, suffered at the hands of the powerful church inquisitors who adamantly rejected his view.

As egocentric human beings, we like to think everything revolves around us. However, we really are not the center of the universe; God's order in the physical universe parallels a spiritual reality: We were all created to revolve around the Son. In fact, when God sends the New Jerusalem at the end of time, Scripture prophesies that there will be "no need of the sun or of the moon to shine in it, for the glory of God illuminated it. The Lamb is its light" (Rev. 21:23). Christ Himself will be the light around which we all revolve. At that time, all of creation will be *huios* centered (Son centered).

Today, the bright yellow sunflowers that grow in our gardens are heliocentric. Their Greek name is *helianthus,* which springs from two words: *helios* meaning "sun" and *anthos* meaning "flower."[1] The French word for sunflower is *tournesol,* which literally means "to turn with the sun." Sunflowers are an amazing breed of flowers since they are beautiful to behold, follow the sun and provide sustenance to living creatures. Birds, animals and human beings love to snack on their crunchy seeds.

In our garden of friends, sunflowers exhibit characteristics similar to nature's sunflower. They

- Stand strong
- Seek the Son
- Sow seed

The sunflowers in our heart's garden can help us radically change our outlook by becoming like sunflowers who stand tall, keep our eyes on the Son of God and sow His seed to a hungry world.

The Garden in My Heart

As believers, we should all strive to be the sunflowers in God's garden: staying spiritually strong, turning our eyes toward Christ and generously feeding those who are spiritually starving.

Stands Strong

My friend Jennifer has stood strong as a sunflower for many years. Though she is not physically tall, in many ways she's a spiritual giant. A petite redhead, Jenn quietly but firmly stands on the Lord's promises, even when times are tough. Several years ago, she and her husband got involved in a business lawsuit that threatened to destroy their financial stability. Jennifer never complained or questioned God's sovereignty during the months and years of legal struggles. She backed her husband unquestioningly and stood firm in her faith. When I'd ask how things were going, rather than complaining, she'd say, "God is good. I just keep praying."

> *Happiness is like your shadow. Run after it and you will never catch it, but keep your face to the sun and it will follow you.*
>
> ANONYMOUS

In the midst of terrible turmoil, Jenn continued to serve in ministry. She has long mentored women who lead small groups; and despite legal and financial difficulties, she stands strong as a godly Titus 2 woman: "Reverent in behavior, not slanderers, not given to much wine, teachers of good things" (Titus 2:3). So many women in our church's Bible study, including me, have been strengthened in the faith because of Jenn's willingness to stand beside them. Whether I'm battling depression, a migraine or uncertain finances, Jennifer loyally stands beside me, a strong, shining example of Christ's love.

Seeks the Son

Sunflowers not only stand strong, but they also are phototropic, turning their heads to follow the sun's light across the sky, looking east in the morning and ending the day facing the setting sun in the west. Sunflower friends are known for "looking unto Jesus, the author and finisher of our faith" (Heb. 12:2). My friend Sondra is like this. When she lost her daughter to cancer several years ago, she kept her eyes on Jesus. She continued to stay focused on Christ, never giving in to the despair that could have overwhelmed her. Now she is fighting cancer in her own body and, even when the news from oncologists seems bad, her gaze has never shifted from her Savior. She, her husband and their eldest daughter have focused on Christ as they again walk through the valley of the shadow of death. They have accepted that, rather than ministering to the helpless and homeless as they once did with their rock band, their new ministry is to show others the love of Christ in the hospitals and doctor's offices where Sondra receives treatment.

Sows the Seed

Sunflowers are well known for providing nutritious seeds that can be used as food products or to make oil. Another friend of mine, Nancy, is committed to sowing the nutritious seed of God's Word in foreign lands. An ex-law enforcement officer with karate training, Nancy spent the last few years taking biblical counseling classes with an eye to helping the women in our church. While she was training to spread God's Word to women at home, Nancy had no idea that one day she would spread the seed of God's Word even further. Nancy's heart was moved when she heard about the persecuted church in Asia. She asked a friend, "What can I do to help them?" He encouraged her to begin by interceding in prayer, knowing that God would reveal any other action she should take.

For months Nancy prayed for the church and for those willing to risk their lives for the sake of the gospel. She was particularly moved when she heard of a man I'll call James who was arrested and tortured for preaching to his countrymen. She thought, If he's willing to lose his life for Christ, I'm willing to put my life on the line. So Nancy became a smuggler, going alone into a foreign country to carry contraband Christian literature and Bibles to those hungry for God's Word. God has watched over Nancy on her dangerous trek and has allowed her to complete her mission to a people hungry for spiritual sustenance.

We won't all have an opportunity to smuggle Bibles into Third World countries, but we can all be like sunflowers, sowing the seed of God's Word in our neighborhoods, businesses, schools and towns.

In God's Garden

Mary, the mother of Jesus, stands out as a sunflower in God's garden. Warren Wiersbe said, "When it comes to Mary, people tend to go to one of two extremes. They either magnify her so much that Jesus takes second place, or they ignore her and fail to give her the esteem she deserves."[2] While she was not God, she was a godly woman whom the Bible uses as an example of faithfulness.

Humble Are Exalted

Perhaps one of the reasons Mary stands tall in Scripture is that she was truly humble. The word "humble" has two connotations: (1) of low standing in a hierarchy or social setting; (2) a freedom from arrogance; a humble spirit. Mary was humble in both ways. She was low on the social scale, even though she was a descendant of King David. And the fact that she was a peasant from Nazareth tells us that she came from the wrong side of the tracks. Nazareth was a frontier town in Galilee and had a bad reputation for immorality and false worship because the people there lived so close to the pagan Gentiles. Even Nathanael, one of Jesus' disciples asked, "Can anything good come out of Nazareth?" (John 1:46).

Obedient Are Blessed

However, Mary wasn't just humble socially; she was also humble in spirit. When the angel Gabriel came to announce that Mary would miraculously bear the Messiah, he called her "highly favored one" (Luke 1:28). This term could be translated as "endued with grace"[3] Her son James could have been thinking of his mother when he wrote, "God resists the proud, but gives grace to the humble" (Jas. 4:6). One reason Mary was chosen to stand tall among women was because she walked in humility and kept herself Son-centered.

Scripture tells how Mary kept her eyes on Christ through obedience to God. When Gabriel announced that Mary would conceive and bear Jesus in her womb through the power of the Holy Spirit, Mary didn't argue with the angel. She simply obeyed, saying, "Behold the maidservant of the Lord! Let it be to me according to your word" (Luke 1:38). Mary's example teaches us that a Christ-centered woman is one who is obedient in following God's Word. Samuel Dickey Gordon said, "Obedience is the eye of the spirit. Failure to obey dims and dulls the spiritual understanding."[4]

Believers See God

Mary, like a sunflower, sowed seeds of faith throughout her life. There is no indication that she, unlike the rest of her family, ever doubted Christ's deity. In fact, she even asked Him to perform His first recorded miracle at a wedding in Cana (see John 2:2-11). Out of respect for her, Jesus turned water into wine. And Mary stayed faithful unto the cross. We know she stood until the bitter end on the hill of Golgotha and watched the suffering of her Son and Savior (see John 19:25). The last time she is mentioned in Scripture she is found in the Upper Room, waiting for the promised Holy Spirit to empower His disciples for witnessing (see Acts 1:14). How wonderful that Mary, who gave birth to Jesus through the power of the Holy Spirit, would ultimately be indwelt with the Holy Spirit at Pentecost. *Nelson's Bible Dictionary* tells us that Mary "stands as the first of the redeemed and as the flagship of humanity itself. She is our enduring example for faith, service to God, and a life of righteousness."[5] Truly, she was a bright sunflower in God's garden.

How Does Your Garden Grow?

To some of our friends we may be a rose, to others a lily or to others a forget-me-not. However, I believe that all believers ought to strive to be sunflowers in God's garden by following some simple steps.

Stake to the Savior

Because sunflowers grow so tall and carry so many seeds, botanists warn against allowing top-heavy sunflowers to fall over. One expert suggests, "When planting taller sunflower varieties, stake the flowers as they grow. Early in the growth stage, place a pole at the base of the stalk. As the stem grows, use twine or soft ties to secure it to the stake every 6 inches or so."[6]

So, too, Christians who want to grow tall should bind themselves to the wooden cross of Christ. Jesus said, "Whoever desires to come after Me, let him deny himself, and take up his cross, and follow Me. For whoever desires to save his life will lose it, but whoever loses his life for My sake and the gospel's will save it" (Mark 8:34-35). Thomas á Kempis wisely said, "In the cross is health, in the cross is life, in the cross is protection from enemies, in the cross is heavenly sweetness, in the cross strength of mind, in the cross joy of the Spirit, in the cross the height of virtue, in the cross perfection of holiness. There is no health of the soul, no hope of eternal life, save in the cross."[7] As a follower of Christ, stake yourself to the Savior by taking up your cross and following Him. When you do, you'll grow tall in your faith.

Saturate in Sunshine

For sunflowers to grow best, "choose a location that gets full sun all day."[8] As bright flowers in God's garden, we grow best when we saturate ourselves in God's sunshine through acts of worship.

The word "worship" has several meanings: "to kiss toward"; "to draw near"; "to pay homage."[9] The Bible tells us to "Kiss the Son, lest He be angry" (Ps. 2:12). Paul explains how to do this: "Be filled with the Spirit, speaking to one another in psalms and hymns and spiritual songs, singing and making melody in your heart to the Lord" (Eph. 5:18-19). Singing God's praises out loud or in our hearts, whether we have the voice of an angel or croak like a bullfrog, is like offering our God the kiss of true love.

> *If we are followers of God, we cannot take the initiative, we cannot choose our own work or say what we will do; we have not to find our way at all, we have just to follow.*
>
> OSWALD CHAMBERS

While spiritual sunflowers gladly worship the Lord, a time will come when those who have not followed Christ will be compelled to worship Him. Revelation 13:8 tells us, "All who dwell on the earth will worship him, whose names have not been written in the Book of Life of the Lamb slain from the foundation of the world." God has given us the choice: We can choose to worship Him now willingly and grow as a beautiful flower in His eternal garden or we can worship Him later under compulsion as we face an eternity without Him.

Scatter Seed

The common sunflower has long been associated with humans, who have cultivated it not just for its beauty but also for the nutrition it provides. Nearly 3,000 years ago, Native Americans in the western United States began domesticating sunflowers for food production by scattering the seeds by hand.

Jesus told a parable that reveals that He expects His followers to also scatter spiritual seed. "The kingdom of God is as if a man should scatter seed on the ground, and should sleep by night and rise by day, and the seed should sprout and grow, he himself does not know how" (Mark 4:26-27). Most commentators agree that the man spoken of in this parable symbolizes redeemed humans who, once they receive the seed of God's Word, are expected to pass it on to others. Herbert Lockyer said of the sower, "He knows that without any interference on his part, all unknown to him the seed will pass through the stages of its natural development. The mysterious workings of God may be beyond our understanding but in this we rest—that although He often hides Himself, His purposes are ripening."[10] The moral of the parable is that we who believe should faithfully scatter the seed of God's Word and leave the results to Him. Paul reminded the Corinthians that while some may plant spiritual seed and others water it, it is "God who gives the increase" (1 Cor. 3:7). I pray that the flowers in God's garden will increase because we scatter the seed of His Word.

There are so many more flowers in God's garden that I could speak of: the perennial plants who faithfully keep growing, like Christy, Patti and Robyn; the exotic plants, like Marta, who make the world such an interesting place to be; the flowering ground cover, like Pat and Tracey, who flourish by humbly working behind the scenes.

You might ask which of God's flowers is most beautiful. My answer: All of them! I pray that, having read this book, you'll look at your friends with new eyes and see each of them as God-given fragrant flowers adorning your life. I pray that you'll help them to see themselves as God sees them. As He proclaimed through the prophet Ezekiel, "I made you thrive like a plant in the field; and you grew, matured, and became very beautiful" (Ezek. 16:7). May you become even more beautiful as you grow and mature in your love for the Lord and your love for the ladies in your garden of friends.

> *As the earth revolves around the sun, so should our lives also revolve around the Son.*
>
> ZIG ZIGLAR

Digging Deeper

1. Journal about some of the ways our society encourages us to be egocentric, thinking the world revolves around us. Describe how this distracts us from being Son centered.

2. Sunflowers follow the sun. As a spiritual sunflower, what problem or preoccupation is causing you to take your eyes off the Son?

3. Read Acts 28:27 and then explain what happens to those who lose their spiritual focus.

4. Rewrite the following Scripture into a personal prayer, asking God to give you eyes to see the spiritual truth of His Word and apply it to your life:

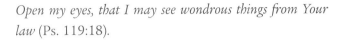

Open my eyes, that I may see wondrous things from Your law (Ps. 119:18).

5. We learned that, along with following the Son, spiritual sunflowers should scatter the seed of His Word. With whom will you share this life-giving seed?

❏ Neighbor
❏ School buddies
❏ Husband
❏ Children
❏ Coworkers
❏ Other _____

6. Describe how viewing your friends as flowers in God's garden has helped you to love and appreciate them more.

Endnotes

Chapter 1

1. "10 Things Your Teen Won't Tell You . . . but She Did Tell Me," *Ladies' Home Journal* online. http://www.lhj.com (accessed January 18, 2005).
2. While all of my personal stories are true, I've changed some names to protect privacy.
3. Mark Altrogge, "I Stand In Awe," 1990, Mercy Publishing.
4. *Vine's Expository Dictionary of New Testament Words,* Biblesoft PC Study Bible, Version 4.2b, © 1988-2004, s.v. "follow."
5. Ibid., s.v. "believe."
6. *Bible Illustrator for Windows,* Version 3.0f, © 1990-98, Parsons Technology, index #304-305, "The Transforming Power of Friendship."

Chapter 2

1. *Strongs Greek/Hebrew Definitions*, Biblesoft PC Study Bible, Version 4.2b, © 1988-2004, s.v. "paradise."
2. *Bible Illustrator for Windows,* Version 3.0f, © 1990-1998, Parsons Technology, index #3517-3519, "Real Empathy."

Chapter 3

1. "Roses FAQ," *The Rosarian*. http://www.rosarian.com (accessed January 4, 2005).

2. *Nelson's Bible Dictionary*, Biblesoft PC Study Bible, Version 4.2b, © 1988-2004, s.v. "thorn."

3. *Bible Illustrator for Windows*, Version 3.0f, © 1990-1998, Parsons Technology, index #304-305, "atonement."

Chapter 4

1. *Bible Illustrator for Windows*, Version 3.0f, © 1990-1998, Parsons Technology, index #4314, "Ignorance of Bible Perilous."

2. *Easton's Bible Dictionary*, Biblesoft PC Study Bible, Version 4.2b, © 1988-2004, s.v. "shushan."

3. "Where Will We Plant Our Lilies?" North American Lily Society. http://www.lilies.org (accessed January 10, 2005).

4· "Mulches," North American Lily Society. http://www.lilies.org (accessed January 10, 2005).

5 *Bible Illustrator for Windows*, index #4314, "Memory Verses: Brokenness."

Chapter 5

1. "Weather History/Traditions" The American Violet Society. http://www.americanvioletsociety.org (accessed March 18, 2004).

2. Lynn Purse, "Color in the Garden: Royal Purple," The Creative Gardener. http://www.creativegardener.com (accessed March 18, 2004).

3. *Nelson's Illustrated Bible Dictionary* and *Vine's Expository Dictionary*, Biblesoft PC Study Bible, Version 4.2b, © 1988-2004, s.v. "humble."

4. *Nelson's Illustrated Bible Dictionary*, Biblesoft PC Study Bible, Version 4.2b, © 1988-2004, s.v. "servant."

5. Herbert Lockyer, *All the Women of the Bible* (Grand Rapids, MI: Zondervan Publishing House, 1963), p. 84.

6. Violet Perfection. http://www.violetperfection.com (accessed March 18, 2005).

7. Maud Grieve, "Violet, Sweet," *A Modern Herbal.* http://www.botanical.com (accessed March 18, 2004).

8. "St. Valentine History/Traditions," American Violet Society. http//www.americanvioletsociety.org (accessed March 18, 2004).

Chapter 6

1. "The Timex Museum, the 1950s." http://www.Timexpo.com (accessed February 4, 2005).

2. *Easton's Bible Dictionary*, Biblesoft PC Study Bible, Version 4.2b, © 1988-2004, s.v. "Eunice."

3. Marianne C. Ophardt, "Geranium Tips." http://www.Tricityherald.com (accessed February 4, 2005).

4. Dale Lindgren, Kim Todd and Loren Giesler, "Diseases of Geranium," revised December 2002, Nebguide. http://www.ianrpubs.unl.edu (accessed February 4, 2005).

Chapter 7

1. *Bible Illustrator for Windows,* Version 3.0f, © 1990-98, Parsons Technology, index #2195, "Need Glasses?"

2. "Daisy, History and Origin, " © 1998. http://www.daisybooks.com (accessed February 22, 2005).

3. "How to Grow Daisies," © 1999-2005 Premier Star. http://www.gardeners net.com (accessed February 22, 2005).

4. Adapted from Mary Ann Perry, "That Pretty April Daisy," 2004. http://www.daisyparadise.com (accessed February 22, 2005).

Chapter 8

1. *Bible Illustrator for Windows,* Version 3.0f, © 1990-98, Parsons Technology, index #2237-2243, "Admire Their Uniqueness."

2. "Annual Flowers: What Are Annuals" © 2005, America's Gardening Resource Inc., Gardeners Supply Company. http://www.gardeners.com (accessed March 18, 2005).

3. "Pansy," Aggie Horticulture. http://www.aggie-horticulture.tamu.edu (accessed March 18, 2005).

4. Karen Russ and Bob Polomski, "Pansies and Johnnie-Jump-Ups," 3-99, Home and Garden Information Center Clemson University. http//www.hgic.clemson.edu (accessed March 18, 2005).

5. Ibid.

6. *Merriam-Webster's Collegiate Dictionary,* 11th Ed., Encyclopaedia Brittanica Online, © 2004, Merriam-Webster, Inc., s.v. "protect."

7. Russ and Polomski, "Pansies and Johnnie-Jump-Ups."

8. Eben E. Rexford, "The Pansy," from Lenore Elizabeth Mulets, *Phyllis' Field Friends Flower Stories,* illustrated by Sophie Schneider (Boston, MA: Colonial Press, 1903), found at "A Celebration of Women Writers," Digital Library, University of Pennsylvania. http://www.digital.library.upenn.edu (accessed June 25, 2005).

Chapter 9

1. *Bible Illustrator for Windows,* Version 3.0f, ©1990-98, Parsons Technology, index #1323, "Friendship: Examples of."

2. Deborah Davis Smith and Michael Whitaker Smith, "Friends" (Brentwood, TN: Meadowgreen Music Company, Birdwing Music).

3. *Easton's Bible Dictionary,* Biblesoft PC Study Bible, Version 4.2b, © 1988-2004, s.v. "anointed."

4. Adapted from "Evangelism." http://www.embracehisgrace.com (accessed March 18, 2005).

5. Elisabeth Ginsburg, "Unforgettable," Backyard Gardener.com. http://www.backyardgardener.com (accessed March 18, 2005).

6. "Forget-Me-Not," 1999-2005 © Premier Star, The Gardener's Network. http://www.gardenersnet.com (accessed March 18, 2005).

7. Lenore Elizabeth Mulets, *Phyllis' Field Friends Flower Stories*, illustrated by Sophie Schneider (Boston: Colonial Press, 1903), found at "A Celebration of Women Writers," Digital Library, University of Pennsylvania. http://www.digital.library.upenn.edu (accessed June 25, 2005).

Chapter 10

1. Adapted from *Two Friends in the Desert.* http://alcohol411.info (accessed December 9, 2004).

2. "The Desert Garden," Huntington Botanical Gardens. http://www.huntington.org (accessed December 9, 2004).

3. *Nelson's Bible Dictionary,* Biblesoft PC Study Bible, Version 4.2b, © 1988-2004, s.v. "Deborah."

4. *Vine's Expository Dictionary of New Testament Words*, Biblesoft PC Study Bible, Version 4.2b, © 1988-2004, s.v. "like-minded."

5. *Bible Illustrator for Windows,* Version 3.0f, © 1990-98, Parsons Technology, index #2407-2416, "Resurrection."

Chapter 11

1. *Bible Illustrator for Windows,* Version 3.0f, © 1990-98, Parsons Technology, index #1314-1316, "Forgiveness, the Crucial Word."

2. Justin M. Norton, "Wildflower Feared Extinct Found in California," ABC News US. http://www.abcnews.go.com (accessed June 25, 2005).

Chapter 12

1. Michael S. Reid, "Sunflower, Produce Facts," October 2004. http://www.postharvest.ucdavis.edu (accessed March 29, 2005).

2. Warren Wiersbe, *Be Compassionate: An Expository Study of Luke 1-13* (Wheaton, IL: Victor Books, 1988), p. 13.

3. *Vine's New Testament Dictionary*, Biblesoft PC Study Bible, Version 4.2b, © 1988-2004, s.v. "favored."

4. *Bible Illustrator for Windows,* Version 3.0f, © 1990-98, Parsons Technology, index #2614-2619, "Obedience."

5. *Nelson Bible Dictionary*, Biblesoft PC Study Bible, Version 4.2b, © 1988-2004, s.v. "Mary."

6. Jeannine Firtzgeralds, "Sunflowers—Growing Sunshine," June 27, 2001, CSU Cooperative Extension. http://www.ext.colostate.edu (accessed March 29, 2005).

7. *Bible Illustrator for Windows*, index #891-892, "Cross of Christ."

8. Firtzgeralds, "Sunflowers—Growing Sunshine."

9. *Vine's New Testament Dictionary,* s.v. "worship."

10. Herbert Lockyer, *All the Parables of the Bible* (Grand Rapids, MI: Zondervan Publishing House, 1963), p. 253.

Enjoy More Resources
By Penny Pierce Rose

Let the words of my mouth and the meditation of my heart be acceptable in Your sight, O LORD. Ps. 19:14

The Pathway Bible Study Series. These Bible studies by Penny Pierce Rose and Lenya Heitzig will take you on in-depth, life-changing spiritual journeys. Ideal for use in daily devotions as well as in group studies, *The Pathway Series* is a perfect fit for today's Christian women. These biblically sound guides will take you on a journey of exploration through God's Word, explain the history, language and culture of the time, and ultimately bring you to a place of spiritual transformation. The first book, *Pathway to God's Treasure: Ephesians* won the Gold Medallion Award for Excellence in Evangelical Christian Literature. Available at Christian bookstores or online stores.

True Identity—The Bible for Women. A 2005 release from Zondervan is a wonderful Bible to keep by your bedside for morning devotionals or at the office for a spiritual pick-me-up. *True Identity* is designed to help women express who they are in Christ in very practical ways. Penny wrote 200 of the "He Is" call-outs scattered throughout the Bible to help you discover who God is and how to respond in your thoughts, attitudes, and actions. Available at Christian bookstores or online stores.

Web: www.pennypiercerose.com • www.hisfootsteps.org